I'M NOT GOING ANYWHERE

I'M NOT GOING ANYWHERE

WRITTEN BY

KELLY LANG

Leopard Entertainment
Hendersonville, Tennessee

Kelly Lang | Leopard Entertainment
PO Box 260
Hendersonville, Tennesse 37077

KellyLang.net

Photo Credit: Michael Jenkins - cover photo and pages 264, 267, 278, 286, 290, 296
Photo credit: Kris Rae Orlowski - pages 207, 234, 288, 289, 298
Editing and book design by Missy Querry
I'm Not Going Anywhere | Kelly Lang -- 1st ed.
ISBN 979-8-4780525-4-6

Printed and bound in the United States of America
Published by Leopard Entertainment

First printing September 2021

I Dedicate This Book To:

My Heavenly Father: *May my telling of this story be pleasing to you and bring comfort to the readers. Thank you for sparing my life and allowing me to live beyond my wildest dreams.*

The love of my life, T.G. Sheppard: *Thank you for loving me unconditionally and completely. Thank you for walking beside me over every mountain and through every valley.*

My beautiful daughters, Payton and Kennedy: *I am so grateful to God for allowing me to be your mother. I love you both with all of my heart.*

My wonderful mother, Nancy Lang: *I adore you and have learned how to be strong from you. Thank you for always being there for me.*

My awesome sister Traci: *I so appreciate the countless hours you have spent teaching me how to live more authentically and helping me to emotionally heal.*

All that are in my life that may not be mentioned within this book: *please don't feel that I have overlooked you. You know how special you are to me, but I only had so many pages.*

CONTENTS

FOREWARD

BY DAME OLIVIA NEWTON-JOHN

I first met lovely Kelly at Barry Gibb's Love Hope Ball in Florida in June 2007 and then again at Barry's house the next day. I was taken by her open personality and we were immediately connected by our journey with breast cancer. Mine having been since 1992, Kelly's was still a fresh memory. We realized we were fellow thrivers and have been friends ever since. There is an unspoken connection with women who share this experience, and Kelly and I have that bond.

She is extremely positive and strong and lives life every day to the fullest with the support of her loving husband T.G. Sheppard, and her children. Through the years we have known each other, Kelly has always been there, even if we don't see each other for long periods of time. We stay connected with phone calls and texts, sharing our lives.

When I was working in Las Vegas, Kelly asked if I would sing a Barry Gibb song with her for her upcoming CD (Throwback). This was so perfect as we both love Barry so much, and we met through him. Thank you Barry.

Kelly has such an original sound, very distinctive, which is key for a singer. I love her voice, and we had fun singing together.

When I was honored to receive my Damehood from Her Majesty the Queen, Kelly had towels made with "Dame Olivia" on them! Soo thoughtful! She sends gifts every now and then...just because. So sweet. We stay in touch, even if months apart. I know she has my back, and I have hers. Upbeat and positive, kind and thoughtful, caring and strong, that is Kelly.

It's important to share our journeys because it helps other women who are on that road to know that they can get through this and they are not alone. Kelly and I share that connection, and I am so grateful for her love and support.

INTRODUCTION

During the pandemic, staying home month after month, I finally decided to clean out our garage. I was overwhelmed opening up each box that had been stacked in there for so many years.

When we had moved into our current house, we hadn't taken the time to unpack hundreds of boxes from our pasts. Not having needed anything in them as of yet, and being the procrastinators we are, they remained in there for way too long. We keep everything! Fan mail, photo albums, baby clothes, cassette tapes, etc... We've both had such full lives, and we couldn't part with the thousands of meaningful trinkets.

Some of the boxes were from my husband, T.G. Sheppard's previous life and career. I saw his music awards and accolades that I never knew existed. We had so much fun talking about each one. He sat and told me stories of each memory.

Some were memorabilia from my music career; Priceless memories that we were able to relive with each other. It was so cool. We enjoyed cleaning everything up and putting the items that meant the most in their proper and labeled boxes.

I ran across old pictures that I've been trying to scan for safety sake and my daughters' school and artwork that I cherish. I put all of these precious momentos in safer containers as well.

Who is this new organized me? I don't even recognize myself. On a good note, we were finally able to put both cars in the garage with extra room to boot!

One of the most surprising things I found was just a bunch of paper I had scribbled on. I almost threw it away, but I decided to read through what some of the pieces had written on them.

For some reason, 16 years earlier, I began to jot down everything that had happened to me during my bout with breast cancer. The doctors mentioned to me that I might want to make a video for my daughters or keep a journal just in case my cancer were to be terminal. I began to note everything. I thought that I might want to write a book to help someone at the time, but I never really pursued it. I must have kept them for some reason, though. I am grateful that I still had those notes, if only to give them to my daughters for future reference.

That night, I told my sweet friend Kim Fannin about how much work we had gotten done in the garage and how proud I was of us finally tackling such a big job. Her response was really surprising. She said she dreamed that

I wrote a book, and it helped a lot of people. Just super random. Or was it?

I let her know that I had found the scribbled notes from my time with cancer and that at the time I wrote them, I didn't think it was book-worthy. She encouraged me to consider looking back at them and then to go forward with how much I've learned since. I thought, "Who would really care about what I have to say?" but I took her advice, so here I am.

I honestly don't have any magical secret or special remedy that I use to get through hard times, but the common thread that I do see running through my life as I read back on my words is that I believe in God; I know He listens to prayers and still loves to work miracles. I am a walking-talking testimony of this. He is the Great Physician, and He healed me.

I know that a positive attitude of gratitude can deliver you from all that ails you.

I've seen the darkest of valleys and I've stood on top of the highest mountains. I know that when life seems to be going great, everything can turn on a dime with one diagnosis. But, I also know that when life seems hopeless, we need to learn to just hold on one more day, because everything can shift for the best in the blink of an eye. We can't change circumstances, but we can be in control of how we handle them.

For those that might not know a lot about me, I may look like a city girl, feminine and ladylike, but let me tell you, I am a country girl from Oklahoma. You can't keep an Okie down. Heck, some would be surprised to know that I have pulled a calf with my bare hands before, and I'd gladly do it again. Having strong country roots in my background also gave me the strength to fight whatever was in my path.

I decided to title my book after a song I wrote many years ago called "I'm Not Going Anywhere." I am so very grateful that many who have heard my song on the Ascension Hospital commercials have written to me saying that my music has been of comfort to them. Perhaps my story here within these pages will do the same.

I wanted to share my journey with you in hopes of helping someone get through their toughest of days. Perhaps you can learn from my mistakes, or maybe my sense of humor can help brighten your spirits a little.

Through the years, I have met so many precious souls that have shared their health crises with me. They mentioned that just seeing how I handled my breast cancer diagnosis and my life thereafter helped them cope by just watching me overcome this disease with a smile. I don't want to give the wrong impression by saying anyone should take my advice on medical treatments. I am no doctor! But what I do want to get across strongly in these pages is that we all need to listen to our own bodies and be proactive with our own health.

I am so grateful that Kim encouraged me to complete this book. I pray that it is seen as light-hearted and entertaining yet serious and helpful. I pray that you can see how with just a change of attitude and learning to change the inner dialog can alter the trajectory of your life. I was scared to write my life story for people to read my personal feelings. Then I realized that I wouldn't be taking my own advice if I stayed in that scary place. I invite you to step out of my comfort zone with me as I share my story, "I'm Not Going Anywhere."

To hear the song "I'm Not Going Anywhere" and watch the video, scan the QR code below:

SCAN ME

More bonus stories, music and videos can be found at the end of each chapter in this book. Scan the code on each page with your camera-equipped smartphone to view the bonus materials. (Most IOS and Android devices can read QR codes by scanning with the built-in camera) If you do not have a QR app on your phone visit your app store and search for QR code reader.

IT'S ONLY MAKE BELIEVE

"**M**rs. Lang," the doctor said to my drowsy mother after just giving birth, "Congratulations! You're now the mother of a beautiful baby girl!" My mother was thrilled to finally have a girl after having had two sons before me. As she came to, she was so excited when they handed her the baby, as she wanted to see me in all my glory. She began to unwrap my blanket and diaper and was in total shock. What she saw was definitely not a girl but a BOY with a thatch of red hair on his head! She promptly called for the nurse to come back in asap. She said, "You said I had a little girl!" The nurse said, "Yes ma'am, you sure did!" Mom said, "well then, what on earth is this?" The nurse quickly grabbed the little boy from my mother as she realized that there had been an obvious mistake. They had accidentally given me to Mrs. Smith, a mother of six other red-headed boys, and a little red-headed boy to my mother. I came into this world switched at birth, and my life has been full of surprises ever since.

I was born January 10, 1967, the fourth child of Nancy and Velton Lang in Oklahoma City, Oklahoma. I am the youngest of their children: Traci, Scott, Mike, and myself.

 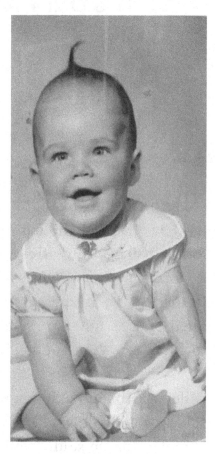

The Lang Gang   *Baby Kelly*

Dad was the manager of a grocery store called Rudy's Red Bud, and mom stayed at home with us kids. We lived a normal middle-class life with nothing too exciting going on until one day... Superstar Conway Twitty entered the grocery store where dad worked and asked to speak to the manager. He needed help in cashing a very large check over the weekend since the banks were closed. My dad helped him do that, and it began a 25-year relationship that would forever change the course of my life.

Conway Twitty's huge hit "It's Only Make Believe" happened to be my parent's love song, so it was quite surreal for them to meet him; rather less, begin a life-long friend and working relationship.

The years developed into Conway needing my dad to go on the road as his road manager. Legend has it that my dad really changed the way many artists began to make more money on concert tours selling tour merchandise, using the techniques he used to help Conway. His charming and charismatic personality had building managers happy to work with him. Other celebrities (Loretta Lynn and George Jones) even wrote in their books about how honest and helpful he was in their careers.

Cowgirl Kelly at 6 years old

Since I was only one year old when dad began working with Conway, I honestly had no idea that he was anything special. Throughout my growing-up years, I really thought it was normal for your parents to take you to work; only my dad's job was backstage at a Conway Twitty concert.

I remember so clearly sitting on the long table beside the stage, looking out at the audience as Conway would take his place. The lights would go out, and the music would begin to play. The mirrored ball that hung from the ceiling would twirl as lights flickered from it, casting little rays over every excited face anticipating his performance. Then the drummer would yell, "Ladies And Gentlemen, please make welcome the High Priest of Country music...The Best Friend A Song Ever Had... COOOOONNNNWAAAYYY TWIIITTTTYYYY!!!!"

No matter how many times I witnessed this phenomenon, it still thrilled me. My heart would pump faster when I heard the audience cheer as Conway began to sing. I knew right then what I wanted to be when I grew up.

I began singing around the house and even wrote my first song in the bathtub at six years old. I recall looking at the Delta faucet as I bathed and thought of the popular song at the time, "Delta Dawn" by Tanya Tucker.

Using her melody, I sang, "Delta Dawn push for shower, then you're gone; push up open, and you'll see that it will run. Push for C and you will freeze, push for H and you will burn. Push up both of them and you will be a mixed-up person". Yeah, I know, pretty weak as a song, but hey, I was only six!

Imagine our surprise as a family when Conway wanted to bring his entire business team from Oklahoma to live in Tennessee, where most artists lived.

In 1975, we drove with several other families within his organization as a caravan (I think there were about 20 of us) to begin a new life in Hendersonville, Tennessee. He promised that we would love this small lake community, and he could really dig into taking his career to another level by being surrounded by other artists. It would allow him more opportunities to be embedded in his career if he lived in *Music City*. So off we went. This move was the greatest opportunity, not only for Conway to be closer to the music industry, but little did I know that it would be life-altering for my future as well.

Velton Lang, Conway Twitty and Kelly

He was right! We loved Hendersonville, and this is where I decided to stay and raise my own family. It is about 20 miles north of Nashville and is enriched with such musical history. Some artists who have lived here include Ricky Skaggs, The Oak Ridge Boys, Johnny and June Cash, Marty Stuart and Connie Smith, Roy Orbison,

Lorrie Morgan, George Jones, Tammy Wynette, and many more. It is nothing to see a well-known celebrity buying groceries at Publix. Everyone in our town is respectful of their privacy and yet proud to call them neighbors.

Looking back, I think I was born to perform. At seven years old, I distinctly remember getting a gooseneck lamp and using it as my spotlight. I sold tickets to my parents and even made backstage passes for them to tape to their shirts. I took a small piece of wood and punctured little holes into the top of it to look like a microphone. I tapped into the sides of it with a hammer and a nail, a K and a star and an L; then used a U nail to attach a long white string to the end of it as the mic chord. I spent many an hour practicing my autograph in anticipation of being asked for it in real life. I would sing to Crystal Gayle records and honestly thought I was her as I slung my long hair from side to side while singing.

I began third grade at Nannie Berry Elementary and met lifelong friends while there. I joined every talent show or play I could get into and was even cast as Alice in *Alice In Wonderland.*

I would roller skate around my parent's carport to all of the music mom would have blaring throughout the house. She mostly played pop music like Gladys Knight, Frankie Valley, Elvis, but of course, there was always Conway. I have to say my mom's love of all types of music undoubtedly gave me my love of all genres and a great appreciation of the power music can play in one's life.

I begged my parents for a piano, but they weren't too sure how much I would really play one. They made a deal with me. If I could learn how to play the guitar (the free guitar a friend was giving away), then they would consider getting me a piano. Well, that's all it took! I began learning the guitar, instantly teaching myself chords from a book and played only by ear. It was time to graduate to my beloved piano!

I was so happy to get my piano, but that came with dreaded lessons. *Ugh*, I hated learning baby steps. I wanted to play full songs! I remember my piano teacher would work so hard on teaching me how to read music notes, but when her husband would come in the room, he would teach me chords and how to play songs faster. She got wind of that and realized I was just playing by ear. I guess you could say that I was officially *fired* by her as a student. Still to this day, I can not read a lick of music; but I cherish the chords I learned. Funny thing, I rarely play either anymore unless I am writing a song. If I choose one instrument over the other, it is the guitar; parents always know best, Lol.

I became immersed within our youth group at First Baptist Church Hendersonville, singing at every bonfire or service I could. I became a follower of Christ and got saved and baptized there at 12 years old and have precious memories from that era in my life. One of my fondest memories of attending church there was when Johnny Cash and June Carter came in late to the service. In not wanting to make a scene, they slid upstairs into the balcony. Keep in mind, it was hot summertime, and they were dressed head to toe in black. I wondered if they might have thought that by dressing in all black they wouldn't be noticed. Boy, were they wrong. Everyone was always so excited to see them.

I was honored to be invited by *The Ralph Emery Show* to perform at twelve years old. Albeit my performance was not the best, it did whet my appetite for more to come. I was so excited when the local paper wrote an article about me. It encouraged me to continue with my dream.

Kelly's promotional picture for her Billboard charting single "Lady, Lady"

I was eventually asked back for repeat performances on Ralph Emery's show and later became a weekly performer, taking country music star Lorrie Morgan's place. So many famous stars got their break on this Nashville based show including the Judds and Dolly Parton

One performance led to another and another. It was so exciting to be asked to sing. I would have sung for a garage door opening if it had asked me!

Conway had a bowling league when I was a kid. There was a restaurant that we would all eat at after their games called The 11th Frame. I loved the live music they played in that smoky club. I asked the manager if he would let me perform there, which led to my first professional gig at $50 a week! I *LOVED* that job. My parents couldn't have stopped my passion for wanting to perform even if they wanted to. I felt bad that some old bitty at church once cornered my sweet mom and said, "Does Kelly mind that you make her sing at bars?" It was quite the opposite. My mother was never the *Stage Mother*. It was always me pushing her to take me to my singing gigs. I was so proud that my mother didn't even offer her an explanation and just walked away.

My parents were always supportive of all of us kids, encouraging us to be whatever we wanted to be, as long as we were happy and treated others with kindness and respect.

My mom was the coolest. She knew that the profession I was choosing would make me need to dress with a little more flare than most kids my age. In my first professional photo shoot, she allowed me to dress much older and sexier than other girls at my school. My friends were totally jealous that I got to wear the latest Candie high-heeled shoes.

Promotional photo wearing her infamous Candies shoes

Mom had a fun sense of humor to her as well. I recall being called into the principal's office one day during gym class in the 7th grade. The principal reluctantly told me that I needed to call home and ask for a change of underwear! *OMG!* I thought how horrifying that was! I must have had my monthly bill come due. But my gym teacher just laughed and said that the word printed on the back of my panties was showing through my white gym shorts. Most moms were buying panties with the days of the week on them....oh not my mom! She bought me some with the word *AVAILABLE* on my backside! We all laugh about it now, but I'm sure I was made fun of at the time.

I am blessed in that, being the youngest kid, my mom was able to travel with me when a prominent booking agent, Tandy Rice at Top Billing, took me under his wing. He began to book me all over the country as an opening act for most of the artists on the charts. I had recorded a song called "Lady Lady" when I was almost 15 years old, and it miraculously made it onto the *Billboard Top 100* chart at #88. It was exhilarating to have this much success at such a young age. At the time, CMT was just beginning, and they needed content to fill up their network. They approached me with the idea of them paying for my first video to accommodate my first hit single. I was allowed to cast a boy I had a crush on to play the cowboy, and right then and there on the tv screen, I had my first kiss!

One important singing engagement I was part of was in 1981 at the two-day festival, *Jamboree In The Hills* in West Virginia. I was in heaven as I walked onto the stage with over 60,000 in attendance. I shared the stage with all of my heroes, including Conway, Hoyt Axton, Alabama, Billy "Crash" Craddock, Merle Haggard, Tom. T. Hall, Emmy Lou Harris, Con Hunley, Bill Monroe, Ray Stevens, and more; but most importantly, a man who was on fire that day on top of the charts with his hit "Party Time," T.G. Sheppard.

He was so charming and sexy. I know this may sound crazy, but I don't remember how we initially met. It had to have been before this day because we already knew each other to say hello after the show. He had been an opening act for Conway in the years previous, so perhaps that was it.

Kelly, T.G. Sheppard and Nancy Lang (mom)
at Jamboree In The Hills

There was something magical that happened that day. I was only 14 years old, and the only star I had in my eyes was to be a performer. What a joy it was to get to share the stage with these legends. In addition to that, as my mom and I were leaving, T.G. leaned in to kiss my cheek goodbye; my little knees literally buckled beneath me. Mom teased me relentlessly all the way home.

Never in a million years would I have ever guessed that he would become such an integral part of my life in the future, but God did.

After a few years passed, T.G. called my house, and spoke to my mom about the possibility of us flying out to L.A. to perform on a network TV show with him called *Fantasy* hosted by Peter Marshall and Leslie Uggams. The show's premise was to give opportunities to people who the stars thought deserved a shot on television. At the time, I was only 16 and was elated at the chance. Mom and I flew to California, and I performed two songs on that show, "I Will Always Love You" and a second song, one of T.G.'s 21 #1 songs called "Faking Love." I sang that as a duet with him. I was so innocent that I didn't even know what making love was, rather less what *faking* love meant.

I was later invited to try out for Ed McMahon's *Star Search*, the equivalent of today's *American Idol*. I was only 18, and at the time, they didn't have the junior division. I was ecstatic yet terrified to compete against the reigning champion Tareva Henderson. She had already won 6 weeks in a row, and here I came along to try and knock her off of the pedestal. I sang "Love Is Alive" by the Judds. To my surprise, the judges scored us exactly the same; for the first time in *Star Search* history, they gave the decision to the audience to break the tie. Well, the audience also tied us!, which led to me coming back to compete against Tareva and another contestant. I sang the Dolly Parton song "Tennessee Homesick Blues" in my 2-piece red fringe outfit, and to my surprise, I beat them both! I then came back a third time and sang "I Will Always Love You" but left that week defeated.

A Funny memory from that era was when I was chosen to be a contestant on Ed McMahon's *Star Search*, I was told to send whatever song I wanted to sing to the music director ahead of time. The only catch was that it had to be edited down to 2 minutes and 30 seconds. My mom had this great idea to help me time it. When I got to Los Angeles to rehearse, the song seemed much shorter than I recalled. He said that my tape was too long and wondered how I had decided where the cut-off was. I innocently told him that my mamma timed it with an egg timer! He said, "You're from Tennessee, aren't you?" Although that is hilarious in hindsight, I was pretty embarrassed at the time.

Looking back at the videos from those shows, I had more desire and spunk than I had talent. I have so much respect for the artistry of the kids on these types of shows today. The pressure of social media is enough to make one so self-conscious. I'm grateful I didn't have that issue on top of the performance nerves. But, what an awesome experience I am forever thankful to have had.

One of the perks I received from performing on national television was the realization that more people knew who I was. A personal and career highlight moment came for me when I went to see Dolly Parton perform at the Opry House after my *Star Search* performance. She got word that I was at her show, and she called me up on the stage to thank me for singing her songs on *Star Search*. My life could have ended with me being a very happy girl right then and there, but God had much bigger plans.

I was graduating from high school, winning the honor as most talented in the class. I was beginning to perform more and more on the now dissolved *Nashville Network* and well on my way to a very successful career.

Scan this code with your camera-equipped smartphone to view the bonus video. (Most IOS and Android devices can read QR phones by scanning with the builtin camera.) If you do not have a QR app on your phone visit your app store and search for QR code reader.

2

ON THE ROAD AGAIN

As I mentioned earlier, my mom played such an important part in helping me to chase my dreams. She always told us that her favorite bible verse was Romans 8:28 *-And we know that in all things God works for the good of those who love Him, who have been called according to His purpose.* She condensed that verse throughout the years to "Everything Happens For The Best." As I look back over my life, I am grateful that she spoke that over me all of the time.

If the timing had been different, and I had not been the youngest, she wouldn't have had the freedom to travel with me. I have such a wonderful and unique relationship with her, very much like sisters rather than mother/daughter. The memories that we shared are unlike what most kids would want with their mother, but my mom was and still is amazing!

To someone looking at a performer, you might only see the artist on stage, all dressed up to sing, perhaps some bling on their clothes for extra effect. You hear the band strike up, and it all sounds like they've played together for years. "Oh, how glamorous the life of a singer must be," one might think. However, what you don't see is the hard work, the hours of travel and staying in not-so-nice hotel rooms, meeting bands right before a show that promised that they already worked on your songs (all the while you know they hadn't). You don't see how many hours of dreaming, rehearsing, shopping for just the right costume for the occasion, and the disappointments that come along with *Show Business*. I lived, ate, and breathed the music business, refusing to give up. I'm so grateful that my mom held my hand through all of the ups and downs.

I had a front-row seat in how *Show Biz* went, just seeing it through my dad's eyes as he worked for Conway Twitty. Dad had met almost every entertainer there was to be met. Honestly, he did not want his daughter to grow up to be in the business,

Kelly and her dad Velton Lang

rather less act like some artists with bad attitudes. Once Dad realized that there was nothing that could be done to stop my desire to be a performer, he laid down serious ground rules for me. I had to be respectful of not only my parents, as all of us kids had to, but he made a serious attempt to make sure I treated *EVERYONE* with the same respect. I had to keep my grades up; I had to keep my weight down. I had to be dolled up at all times when out in public! He was like a football coach. I realized that later in life, some of his strict rules would be to my benefit, but at the time, I thought he was tough on me. He didn't want me to get the *Big Head*. I guess he thought if I was going to be a professional artist, then I was to behave like one. I was an extension of him, and I certainly didn't want to let him down.

Dad struggled with telling me personally that he was proud of me as a singer or if he thought I did a good job onstage. I never doubted his love for me but, I sometimes questioned his faith in my music. It wasn't until fans that he met through Conway, or other artists told me how proud he was of his little girl that I knew how he really felt about my career. Thanks to social media, I still hear from Twitty fans that knew my dad, sharing with me how much he believed in me. It's such a comfort to still hear this so many years after his passing. I wish I had known that earlier. I miss him so much every day. I still feel his presence and hear his advice in my heart. I truly adored him and am honored to have been his daughter.

When I began to sing professionally, it was such a fun time in the music industry. *Urban Cowboy* was just getting ready to hit. As a matter of fact, I recall playing at a club in Nashville on Printer's Alley, and Mickey Gilley was there talking to me about a movie he just filmed with John Travolta. It was all about his club Gilley's. He said it was going to be a big hit and change country music. I honestly didn't believe him at the time, but holy cow!!! He sure

Kelly (12yrs) as Urban Cowgirl

was right. I loved the influence it had on the style of clothes, allowing me to break out my fringe and cowboy hats with pride. I loved that movie with everything that was in me. I adored most songs that played on the radio in that era. In my opinion, country music in the '80s was the ultimate!

Once I was signed to Top Billing Talent Agency, I would get contracts in the mail from them for the upcoming month. For a 14-year-old kid, I was making great money! I just wished I had known about investing back in the day. The paperwork would only include details of how much I was getting paid, half of the deposit upfront, the time of the show, who I was opening the show for, and the buyer's name and address with their phone number. That was it! Keep in mind that we didn't have computers back then for websites, and no GPS to show my mom and me where we were going; heck we didn't even have cell phones to call to get any info or to have in case of an emergency. I can't believe my dad allowed us to go. That's so dangerous when you think about it.

However, my mamma could read a real road map like a pro! She and I would hop into her car and drive from one show to the next without asking questions. I was in awe of her ability to drive for hours and never get tired or get lost. Well, there was that one time when we took a left, and it should have been a right. At dark, she swerved a little bit, trying to figure where she should have turned, and a cop pulled us over. He wanted to make sure why two women were on that dark winding road so late at night, as he warned us that a murderer was on the loose!!! How terrifying!

Although mom was always willing to drive me where I needed to go, she was by *NO* means a typical *Stage Mother*. She is rather shy and reserved but with a wonderful wit. She loves music but never saw herself as a manager type in any way. She has a recurring dream that I got sick and couldn't sing, and she had to take my place! That would be her worst nightmare!

Anytime there might be a problem with collecting money from a buyer, it was teenage *ME* who had to stand up to these people and demand my paycheck. That actually happened a few times. I guess they figured that they could pull a fast one on a kid and her mommy. Oh no! I had spunk and grit to handle all of that stuff, probably more like my dad in that way. I feel like I am a good combination of both of my parents, feminine, and calming like mom is, but have a passion for business and more personality traits like my dad. However, I don't think I look anything like either of them at all. Oh wait, I was switched at birth, so...

One of our favorite things to do on the road was to look for radio towers on the interstate. I'd make her stop at every one so I could go in and ask the local DJ if they'd play my new song; very much like you'd see in *Coal Miner's Daughter*, where Loretta and Doo did the same thing. It was a more simple time compared to now, and that wouldn't be as welcomed today.

We would always get a coke with peanuts and have burping contests along the way while listening to Casey Kasem's *American Top 40* countdown show and betting on who went number 1 that week. This all seemed normal to me. Looking back, I can now see why others might judge their parenting skills by allowing me to get out of school to sing, but to me, my parents were perfect.

My school teachers probably talked about us behind my back as I slid in sideways to school from being on the road. I just *ALWAYS* knew who and what I wanted to be, and I felt that school was in the way of getting to my official life as an entertainer. I don't recommend this to anyone, but it was just the truth for me.

At the start of 9th grade, I had come in from singing on the road to a test the algebra teacher wanted me to take. She told me to take it to the library to complete as the class was already on to another lesson. I sat in that library forever, trying to figure out what all of those symbols meant to no avail. Luckily a friend/substitute teacher came by and helped me with the test. What I didn't know was that it was an aptitude test. Since it looked like I *passed* it with flying colors, the teacher put me into the *A* group when I was clearly not supposed to be there. My dad had to call the principal and explain what I'd done and tell them that his kid wasn't that great in math. How humiliating!

The other time I should have done better in school was in my Senior year. I was on the road every single weekend working and only took easy-breezy classes that last semester just to graduate; I made pretty good grades but was certainly no scholar. I had no intentions of going to college as school couldn't prepare me for my career. However, the thing I didn't take into account was the *ONE* class that I just didn't show up for at all was *CHILD DEVELOPMENT!* That was the *ONLY* class I *FAILED! OOPS!* Sorry kids! Life would teach me that lesson later. Oh, how I wish I had shown up for those invaluable classes.

Funny, many, many years after I graduated, I ran into my old High School principal. I introduced myself. He laughed and said, "No introduction needed." I was amazed by his ability to remember me as he was over thousands of kids throughout his time there. He said, "Average student, average grades, but you excelled in people skills! I'm very proud of how well your career has turned out for you, Kelly." How sweet and what a full-circle moment for me.

Because I started my career at such a young age, I couldn't drive since I wasn't old enough to have my license yet. Mom never complained, not even once. However, there was that time when she was taking me to the *Ralph Emery Morning Show*, and as we were driving in downtown

Nashville at 4:45 am, she admitted that she didn't feel well. I felt her forehead and realized that she had a fever. I felt so bad for her but only realized how bad it was when she said, "Oh look, the sun is already coming up." I said, "Mom, that is the Days Inn sign!" We laughed so hard! Mom is easy to tease and can always take a joke.

Mom and I loved to watch *Days Of Our Lives* and would always tape the shows on the VHS players just in case we couldn't get back in time to watch. One time we were coming home from a concert in Kentucky and realized that we hadn't set the recorder to tape the biggest story of all time - *The wedding of Bo and Hope*!!! By this time I had my license and was driving. Trying to get home to watch the show, I frantically began to speed. A police officer instantly pulled me over. As I rolled down the window, he said, "I hate tattletales. Someone tattled on you and told me to pull you over. If you can tell me a great reason for your speeding, I might just let you off the hook." Oh gosh! I took the *truth shall set you free* approach, and told him all about our need to see our TV show. He laughed and said his wife watched *Days Of Our Lives* too, and that he totally understood. He let us go scott free!!! Oh yeah, we also missed a flight once because of that dang show!

Although it has been a very fun and exciting ride, my career would never have been as much fun without my sidekick. I always loved getting back to the hotels after the shows were over and comparing stories from the evening.

I love taking my mom into the studio with me when I record. She has had such an influence on my love of music, and I enjoy seeing her face light up when I sing her favorite songs. One day while in the studio, my co-producer Buddy Hyatt began calling her Billie. I thought for a second that he didn't realize her name was Nancy. When he called her Billie again, I corrected him. He said, "I know her name is Nancy, but she's like your umbilical cord, so her new name is Billie." So, that's what she answers to now with pride.

She always tells me that she's my biggest fan, but the truth be told, I am hers. And, mom was right that "Everything indeed worked out for the best."

Kelly and Mom (Nancy Lang)

And we know that in all things God works for the good of those who love Him, who have been called according to His purpose.

Romans 8:28

Scan this code with your camera-equipped smartphone to view the bonus video. (Most IOS and Android devices can read QR codes by scanning with the built-in camera) If you do not have a QR app on your phone visit your app store and search for QR code reader.

3

CHOICES AND CONSEQUENCES

For every choice we make in life, there is a circumstance that follows. If I had decided to turn left instead of right, would I have met the same people along the way? Would I have been happier? Oh, how I sometimes wish I could see into a crystal ball. But then again, the idea of the unknown is so exciting. I honestly believe that whatever decisions we make in life, it all turns out as God had intended anyway. I can just see God giggling as we think we are in charge of our lives. Kind of like us as parents, you see your kid running towards something a bit dangerous, but you allow them to anyway, as only then can they learn the lesson for themselves. We all need to be wrapped in bubble wrap and given bumpers for this thing called life.

During my senior year of high school I began dating a man that became my first husband. I should have listened to my gut instinct when it told me not to get married at 19 years old. My parents were so upset and begged me not to do it, but at that age, nothing could have stopped this hard-headed girl who thought she knew everything. I was heartbroken when after hearing of my engagement announcement, my booking agent, Tandy Rice, sent me a letter releasing me as one of his clients. He explained that it was a big mistake for me, and he was disappointed that all of the time he put into my career was just going to be thrown away.

I was devastated by this dismissal and yet was too far into the wedding to back out. I mean, the invitations had already been mailed out. I knew it was wrong to go through with it, but I had made a commitment, and I was determined to prove everyone wrong, even myself. I wonder if I had just stayed the course as a single young woman, would my career have flourished?

In hindsight, I looked very confident on the outside but was too insecure and immature to make such a life-long decision. As an adult now, I wish there was a law to protect people from marrying too young. You have to be 21 to drink; I think you should have to be at least 25 to make a commitment as serious as marriage. I bet there would be a lot less divorce and much happier marriages if that were a law. Nobody's brain is capable of making that big of a decision at 19! I bow down to those who marry young and can stay together, but I personally wish I had lived more of my single life first. I was just looking to grow up and get out of the house as an adult, and this guy asked, so I said yes.

Since I had made this commitment, I was going to do my very best at being a wife. However, I instantly felt that I had lost sight of who I was meant to be. Although I sang a little here or there, the daily grind of just trying to make ends meet was brutal. I began to get very blue and resentful. I was just so different from my husband. No-fault to him, but it was almost as if we spoke two different languages. I am the type of person, though, that I give it my best when I commit to something.

One way that I was still able to be creative was to continue to write songs. Most of them at the time were songs about how "I bet he'd never notice that I'm gone" kind of lyrics. I also was able to sing on *The Ralph Emery Morning Show*, which kept my fires for music still burning. I only made $52.11 each week; clearly not enough to sustain me, but it was still a fun job.

Several years into our marriage, I was invited to become a regular on the popular country music show *Music City Tonight* with hosts Lorianne Crook and Charlie Chase. Other regulars were Shania Twain, T. Graham Brown, Ronnie McDowell, Lisa Stewart, and wouldn't you know it, a full-circle moment, Tareva Henderson.

Yep, the same girl I beat at *Star Search* came and knocked me off my pedestal. I had been singing weekly on the show for about a year. However, when Tareva came in with her amazing big voice, the time slots were given to her. At the time, I admit I was a bit jealous, but in hindsight, she was a much better singer, and I had to acknowledge her unique talent. I am happy to have matured past this and learned that there is enough room for everyone in the business. I am grateful that we are friends to this day. Performing on this show was a tremendous opportunity that I still cherish. It was a great learning experience that I likened to going to college for this young entertainer.

A funny thing happened while I was on that show. One night Charlie Chase yelled for me to come into the office to get a message he needed to give me. He said that Playboy had called wanting to do a spread of ladies in country music and wondered if I'd be interested. I certainly didn't believe him as he was such a jokester, but he gave me the number and told me to check it out for myself. Lo and behold, it was on the up and up. I would never ever have posed for them, but I would be lying if I told you I wasn't super flattered with the offer.

I waited five years to have our first baby Payton Michelle (Michelle is my middle name). She was such a doll. I was so happy to have a little girl, but my ex-husband seemed super disappointed not to have a boy to play sports with. I didn't understand his behavior; I mean, she was perfection. Although I wasn't performing nearly as much as I had in the past, I so enjoyed being her mother. I even wrote several songs for her that later became a collection sold in Cracker Barrel Old Country Store called *Lullaby Country*. She was my little muse.

Although the marriage was beginning to crumble, I still kept trying to make it work. I naively thought that maybe if we had another child, it would improve? We waited four more years to have our second baby, yet another girl named Kennedy Lang (my last name). By that time, I guess my ex just gave up on the idea of having a son and threw himself into the role of coaching her in every soccer game he could get her in. She was a great player, and I was so proud of her ability.

In the meantime, the reason I began singing died. Yes, on June 5, 1993, I woke up to the sad news that Conway Twitty had passed away in Springfield, Missouri, of an aneurysm; this tore out my heart. I will speak of how his passing affected me in a future chapter.

Then, on Feb. 20, 1998, at only 57 years old, my dad, my rock, my hero, died of a brain aneurysm. Never have I been so shaken from anything in my life. He was such a strong man; everyone likened him to John Wayne. I was devastated. It tore my entire family up. I was raw and began to realize how short life really was. It taught me that I had to live life more appreciatively and to be true to myself. Dad appeared to me in a dream soon after and told me that I had to stop fighting with my husband. He basically said life was too precious to be that miserable.

Two years after my dad's passing, and after 14 years of marriage, in August of 2000, I finally got up the courage to dissolve our rocky relationship. We had fought about everything. Seriously, one day, the fight was when I said the sky was a pretty shade of blue, and he argued that it wasn't even blue! I couldn't win. I also realized that, sadly, we were not equally yoked. My spiritual side had kept growing, along with the desire to improve my life. Moving forward with him not having the same aspirations was more than I could bear.

The warnings that I had gotten from my parents came to fruition as I realized my dreams were still alive and well, and he frankly had zero drive to change or improve.

I got to the point that I'd rather be alone than to suffocate without the ability to be what I was created to be. Throughout our relationship, there was never any support of my dream to sing. He hated my music and would begrudgingly attend functions, always embarrassing me when he did. Never once did he tell me if he thought I was pretty nor tell me if he was proud of me. These are things that I needed to hear. After a very painful divorce, I pieced my life back together, but this time as a single mother of two little girls, ages five and nine.

After several months as a single woman (my ex had already gotten remarried and was expecting a baby), I ran into an old friend of my mom's at a party at Mario's Italian Restaurant in Nashville, who asked how I had been. Since it had been a long time since seeing her, she was surprised to hear that I was divorced. She proceeded to tell me that T.G. Sheppard was recently single. Now that's weird in itself since I hadn't seen or heard his name in probably six or seven years. The most strange thing is that this friend of mom's was T.G.'s ex-wife!

Two weeks later, while returning to take my mom and sister home from being in the recording studio with me, mom's home phone rang. I said, "Hello." The voice on the other end said, "Kelly? This is your first love." Since I had never spoken to him on the phone before, I had no idea who this could be. He said, "This is T.G. I'm calling to say I'm so sorry about your dad's passing." T.G. had been in business with dad in a t-shirt company years before. They had become friends during the many hours spent together while traveling on the road when he toured with Conway.

He was passing through town and wanted to know if I'd be open to having a drink with him to catch up. How weird and exciting, I thought. My mind began to think back to that night I ran into his ex. Could she have prompted his call? Maybe? But I was thrilled nonetheless. I was a bit less excited when he said that he and his band were at *HOOTERS* and wanted me to meet him there. Of course, I was appalled...all the while freshening up my lipstick as I was running out of the door. My sister Traci and mom were not having me going alone. They insisted on joining me for this crazy moment. I was so nervous! Why? I had performed on tv shows with him and had been around him on dozens of occasions, but I was shaking like a leaf, thinking that this was something different. T.G. was waiting for us inside, and as many times before, he was the perfect gentleman. We all just drank water and talked for about an hour. I remember him asking me how long my hair was; it was braided into a bun. He said he loves long hair on women. (Funny that he asked me that as he now prefers my hair short.)

We all went out to his black Excursion to listen to what I had just recorded that day in the studio. He had never known that I was a writer, so I was nervous about bearing that part of myself to him. To my thrill, he was super impressed! Then, something strange happened to me. I began to look at him differently. Not as a music comrade but as an adult attraction. I noticed how gorgeous his skin was. I loved seeing his grey hair peeping from above his shirt. I mean, he was single; I was an adult and single, but what if he didn't see me in that way?

As we were leaving, He hugged me, (yes my knees buckled again), and he whispered in my ear. "If I were to call you for a date, would you go?" Holy cow! *WHAT??* Of course, I said yes.

Kelly and T.G. Sheppard - first date

On our first *date*, T.G. took me to Kobe Japanese Steakhouse. Afterward, we drove around looking at Christmas lights, and he showed mc all of the places where he once lived before taking me back to my apartment. He admitted to always having a crush on me, but as the gentleman he was, he would never have acted upon that. He was leaving for Mississippi the next day to sing and getting on his tour bus that evening for the drive down. He asked if I'd like to join him to see his show. Since the kids were at their dads for the weekend, I began to consider going with him. I was excited but precautious; I mentioned it to my mom, and she was concerned. What would people think?! He was older than me, and she warned that he would probably not have innocent intentions. She was worried about my reputation. I decided to go with my gut instinct anyway, and I'm so glad I did.

That evening was magical. We spent the entire night just talking. Honestly, just talking! He wanted to know everything there was to know about me. We sat on the floor in the back of his bus talking about music, mutual friends, our divorces, past shows we had done together, my dad, Conway. You name it; we covered all topics. Nothing physical happened, but something was happening in my heart, that's for sure. In between the soundcheck and the show, T.G. hugged me and squeezed my hand three times. He was truly shocked that I squeezed his hand back four times. The significance of this was surreal. My dad had always done this to us kids, signifying three squeezes as *I LOVE YOU*, and four squeezes meant *I LOVE YOU TOO*. Apparently, that was something T.G. had always done and was testing the waters with me to see if I knew his secret code. Sure enough, I must have shocked him because he was surprised with my response. I felt that he was falling for me without ever saying the actual words.

However, I was beginning to worry that he might not be attracted to me as a grown woman. Perhaps he couldn't get past the fact that he'd known me as such a young girl. It took him three long weeks just to kiss me. I later teased him about it. He mentioned that he was very intimidated to kiss me. He didn't want to disappoint me since I had told him he was my secret crush from many years before. One day I had an appointment in downtown Nashville, and on the way inside, he stopped me on a sidewalk and kissed me for real. Not much of a romantic place, but at least we had crossed that hurdle.

I love how romantic T.G. is. I craved that in my life as I am a romantic too, and that was something clearly missing in my previous marriage. One thing that he and I do is to leave a coin in places that we want to remember. For instance, after that first kiss, we placed a quarter in the crack of the sidewalk; so if we ever want to relive that exact feeling, we can retrieve the coin and kind of step back in time. We now have coins at Graceland on the wall, at the Titan's stadium, and of course Hooters etc.... We get such a kick when we can find the coin again. It is like a touchstone proving we were here once before. I even wrote a song about it called "When We Loved Here."

It's funny; I am nothing like anyone he's ever known. I was a bit of a firecracker and never let him get by with anything. I was really falling hard for him, but when he tried to pull back a little by saying, "You know, don't get your feelings hurt if I don't call you as much as you'd hope, I'm a very busy man." That made me a little mad, so I replied with a cocky answer saying, "I too am very busy, so don't be mad if when you call, that I don't answer." He said he loved my spunk and sense of humor.

A long while later, I asked Diana, T.G.'s first wife, why she told me he was single. I wondered if it was her that tried to fix us up? She told me that she had always liked me and, although they had not worked out, that of all the women she could have seen him with, I was the only one she would approve of. She admitted dropping that hint to him in hopes he would be open to us dating. How kind it was of her to be so open-minded and wanting him to be happy.

I was concerned about introducing him to my young daughters until I knew it might be something serious. I had only spent time with him when my girls were at their dad's. It was such a great diversion to spend quality time with them when I had them and also quality time with him when they were away. It was almost like I was leading an exciting double life.

T.G. was 56 when we began dating, and if I were to be completely honest with myself, I sure wouldn't want to be raising someone else's kids at that era in my life. I was worried that I would fall totally in love with this man only to lose him to the idea of him taking us on as a family. Payton seemed to like him right away, but Kennedy, being more of a daddy's girl, well, I had some convincing to do. I realized it would be fine when I saw her sitting beside him on the couch, and I overheard her telling him that she was out of Bonnie Belle lip gloss and panties and that he needed to help her get some new ones. I thought it was adorable of him to take her shopping at Walmart. She made him stand several feet away as she picked out her new Barbie panties.

He was still trying to figure out if this was a lifestyle he wanted when he invited us and several other friends to join him on a trip to Disneyworld. We were so excited. I was worried that Kennedy, having been treated for strep throat earlier in the week and still on antibiotics, would be okay to go. He insisted, saying she could sleep in the bus bunk till we got there. Poor baby was fine when the Tylenol was flowing in her but didn't do so well when it wore off.

T.G. had wanted to be the superhero and fed both girls candy and cookies throughout the day, even riding most of the rides with all of us. At dinnertime, he held a five-year-old, snaggle-toothed Kennedy in his arms and asked if she had a good time. She instantly threw up Oreo cookies all down his perfectly pressed, nice button-down shirt! Anyone that knows T.G. knows how finicky he is about his clothes. They have to be ironed and look crisp and fresh. This must have thrown him over the edge as he was seriously traumatized. I thought for sure that this would be a deal-breaker.

When we got back home from Florida, I didn't see him for weeks. I was so very sad. I mean, I couldn't blame him. They were both high-maintenance little girls. I knew I was falling in love with him, but I was worried it was too much for him to take on. After a while, he called me and just picked up where we left off, later admitting he had to wrap his head around the responsibility of taking us on as a unit. He said he couldn't stay away from me and was missing our time together. Whew!

Scan this code with your camera-equipped smartphone to view the bonus video. (Most IOS and Android devices can read QR codes by scanning with the built-in camera.) If you do not have a QR app on your phone visit your app store and search for QR code reader.

4

@$#! OR GET OFF THE COUCH

As I mentioned before, I had always been fond of T.G. and had total respect for his business sense. He was such a source of comfort for my children and me. Each day that went by, I fell more and more in love with him.

It did seem however, that as the years went by, we weren't anywhere closer to the altar. I tried to be understanding as T.G. explained that he was in a different place than I was in his life. He had gone through two divorces and had begun life as a free and single man when I came along. I had a lot of responsibilities, and my life was not simple in any way.

I loved that he was a stable fixture in our lives after so many years, but I have to admit that just dating him wasn't enough for me any longer. We began to get into little spats more and more often. I totally resented his time away from me while working in Memphis with his family on a now-failed business. We always seemed to have too much distance between us. He gave me a bit of hope when he decided to rent a home in Hendersonville, but since we never lived together, I craved all the time I could have with him during the day. I began to resent the times that he did make it back to Hendersonville (from performing on the road or from spending so much time in Memphis), that every Sunday (which I craved that day off with him), he always wanted to watch Nascar races, *GOOD GRIEF!* How I hated that. I knew that he had a love for Nascar as he was part of the Folgers Racing Team in earlier years, but *hello*?? It was my worst nightmare. I just wanted quality time with him, and I had to spend every Sunday watching cars go round and round.

At that point, I had given him a few ultimatums. "If you don't want a future with me, then get off of my couch and let me move on with my life!" A funny side note, in one of our arguments, I was looking for a new sofa. He kindly bought my couch and called it an *engagement couch* to shut me up, I guess. He sat on it long enough that I think he figured we had joint custody. Even if I wanted to start a new life with anyone else, he didn't seem to want to leave my couch!

This routine went on for way too long. I wasn't getting any younger, and he sure wasn't either. Speaking of age, yes, we have a 23 year age difference. I want it on record that our age difference is one of the many things I love about our relationship. I wouldn't recommend it for just anyone, but it certainly works for us. People have been so rude to us about the age difference. Some have said, "He's so much older, what if he gets sick? You'll have to take care of him!" Strangely enough, I am the one that eventually got sick, and he had to take care of me! It's called sickness and health, and we took that commitment to heart. We've been on one long power date since the very beginning.

One of my favorite things about T.G. is the knowledge he has gained from everything he has experienced in his life. He has been so helpful in walking me through concerns I may encounter in my career and raising children. I feel safe knowing that if he can get through certain things, then I can too. I love his worldliness. I love that he is a dreamer, and he is always encouraging me to dream bigger for myself.

I also loved the businessman that he was and still is. However, I began to see life changing around him. The music business was way different than it was when he was on top of the charts. Money was still flying out of the window as if he was still singing in large arenas. As a frugal partner, I began to offer suggestions on how he could begin to save money. I was truly worried about how any one person could have that much financial responsibility on his shoulders. It was overwhelming to me. He was sometimes performing on the road just to make sure his band members could work; many times, he would make less than they did after expenses were paid.

There was also a concern over some properties that once were a tax shelter; they no longer held this status and had started to drain him dry. Also, he had to go through a lawsuit costing him so much in lawyer fees around this time. At the end of the day, I talked him into filing for bankruptcy. There was just no way out of it. We were so worried that it would ruin his stellar reputation and were relieved that it never made the newspapers.

This time was very depressing for both of us, as we had so enjoyed the finer things in life. As a couple, we decided to really hunker down and streamline all expenses. We ate a lot of tuna fish and dollar cheeseburgers at McDonalds. I was in it for the long haul. I knew if we were smart with our money, he would be able to pull through this difficult time. The one thing he said he learned from going through this period is that he knew beyond a shadow of a doubt that I was not there for his money. I already knew that, but I'm glad he found comfort in realizing it himself. When you have fame in your life, you tend to question everyone's motives.

I realized that T.G. had become more dependent on me after that rough patch. Looking back, we often mention how appreciative we were to have gone through that together. We learned not to take anything for granted.

I'm so grateful to say that at the time of writing this book, we've worked super hard on saving our money, paid off all of our bills, began a debt-free lifestyle, have come back stronger than ever and been able to live for several years in our dream home. I had strong credit, and he had a good income. We sure made a great team.

We dated a total of seven long years! I have never waited that long for anything. He taught me patience, that's for sure. In hindsight, I'm not quite sure if things would have worked out if we had married any earlier. It was too much of a financial mess, and my daughters, as sweet as they were, were quite a handful.

Kelly, T.G., Payton and Kennedy

T.G. had always wanted daughters, but he hadn't figured on raising them in his 60's. He was wonderful to the girls. He called them every afternoon to ask how their day was at school and would reward them for helping me around the house. I used to love it when he would try and help Kennedy with her math skills. He would ask her to figure out problems, like, "If Joe had four dimes but gave one to Mary and she had three pennies to add to it, how much would Mary have?" I loved how the girls clung to him as if he was already their bonus dad, but it also scared me that they were getting too close.

I saw what a great father he was beginning to turn into for them. I wanted to have him as a permanent fixture in our lives, but he was seriously afraid of commitment; I found myself constantly frustrated. I can't wait to tell you how this marriage unfolded in an upcoming chapter... just hang on!

Scan this code with your camera-equipped smartphone to view the bonus video. (Most IOS and Android devices can read QR codes by scanning with the built-in camera) If you do not have a QR app on your phone visit your app store and search for QR code reader.

SCAN ME

5

REBRANDING

As a single mother, I soon realized the need to recreate myself and try something new to make a living. Although I had always continued to write songs, I hadn't been working in the music business in quite a long while and breaking back into that would be quite a challenge.

I looked into every possibility that would be an exciting new chapter and opportunity that would allow me to stay at home with my daughters as much as possible. I didn't want anything to disrupt their already changing lives any more than I had to.

Around this time, T.G. had bought me an oil painting kit. I was confused as to why he thought I'd want to paint. I'd never shown interest in that before, but he felt that since my mom and brother could paint, I probably could do the same. I didn't want to let him down, so I began the process of putting oils on a tiny canvas for a start. My first painting was a gift for T.G., an aerial view of a coffee cup. I thought that was the best idea since he was one of the writers of the Folgers Coffee commercial, "The Best Part Of Waking Up Is Folgers In Your Cup."

Kelly's first painting.

To my surprise, when I went to get it framed for him, the lady at the shop tried to buy it from me! I politely declined but agreed to sell her another one. That sale led to others wanting this tiny painting of a coffee cup. I soon realized that painting was just another artistic form of expression and began joining other artists in free-form classes. I started to attract people from social media that wanted to purchase paintings from me. I then would take orders from people asking me to paint their pets; this became a fun passion since I've always been an animal lover. I'm so proud that some of my pet portraits hang in famous homes, including Dame Olivia Newton-John and Sir Barry Gibb. I have also painted Larry the Cable Guy's dog and later Oprah Winfrey's beloved Sadie.

Oprah's dog Sadie

Sir Barry Gibb's dog Ziggy.

Brutus

Being commissioned to paint for someone is tremendously stressful, and I began to get too nervous in trying to please the clients. I started to lose my joy in painting. Although it financially helped me through some tough times, I now only paint for mere enjoyment.

I had always loved real estate. The idea of buying and flipping houses seemed exciting. I had been renting an apartment but decided to try my hand at getting my real estate license. I had studied hard with T.G.'s help, and I was ecstatic when I passed the test on the first try. Doing so gave me extreme confidence in my ability as a businesswoman. My very first transaction was a condo I had bought for myself. I never even got to the place where flipping properties was an option, as I was so tight on cash, the idea of buying other homes was too scary for me. I started to sell a few houses but quickly realized that I needed to leave real estate to the professionals.

Around this same time, I began a spray tanning company called Tan-Terrific out of my house. I sold my wedding ring to buy the equipment. It became pretty successful. However, I soon realized that it would be a short-lived job for me when an older lady wanted me to tan under her butt cheek line; then proceeded to pass gas on me. Next...

A strange thing happened during the course of this time in my life. While attending a boring real estate class, during a lunch break, a lady approached me and said, "Aren't you Kelly Lang, the singer and songwriter?" I replied, "Yes." She proceeded to tell me that she remembered reading about my music career in the newspaper. She was surprised to see me in a real estate class and was also a little forward to tell me that she had prayed for me when she read the article. How weird, I thought. She said that this was not where God had intended me to be and that I needed to go back to my music. Wow, thanks lady. As if it were just that easy!

I made a decision not to pursue my real estate career any further. It just wasn't for me. I'm way more the creative type, and I got so anxiety-ridden with each transaction.

Strangely enough, about the time I decided to let go of my license, I ran into that same praying lady I had met at the class before in the clothes department at Target. She proceeded to tell me that she was hosting a bible study at a friend's house, and she wanted me to come by for some prayer time. At that point, I felt so lost that I needed all of the prayers anyone was offering, so I agreed to go.

When I arrived at the tiny white farmhouse, the girls began laying hands on me. They asked for God to show me the way back towards my musical career and that He would allow my music to be heard all over the world. Truthfully, I thought they were nuts! I mean, at that time, it was unheard of for a 35-year-old single mother of two to even consider this challenge. Social media was becoming more popular, but this seemed a little too far-fetched. As I left to go home to pack for a beach vacation the next day, I felt stupid even mentioning this situation to T.G., but I'm sure glad I did.

The very next day, while walking through a store in Florida, T.G.'s phone rang. A bus driver he had hired only a few times called to say that he had heard a demo CD of mine that T.G. had left on the bus. The bus driver took it upon himself to share my music with a newly developed record label called Destiny Row Records. He said that the head of talent was so impressed with my music that she wanted to sign me asap. She had mentioned that when he handed her my CD, she felt a shock and actually dropped it.

I had recently been writing some new music and had recorded it. One song was called "Goodbye Darlin'," which I wrote in honor of my late friend and mentor Conway Twitty. I remember having dinner with T.G. one night, and the conversation was all about our memories with Conway. We talked about wondering how he would have felt about us dating and joked that maybe he and my dad were up there putting us together. We both mentioned how much we missed them and what a loss it was for the music industry. I told T.G. how much I regretted never telling Conway how much he meant to me. I honestly was so sad that night.

As we parted ways, on the way home from dinner, this song started coming to me. A melody I had never heard before began ringing in my head. Lyrics about Conway kept haunting me on the 2-hour ride home. T.G. lived in Knoxville, Tennessee, about four hours away from where I lived. On occasion, we would meet for dinner halfway, which was great on this particular night because it gave me the time to work on this song as I was driving. The lyrics and music were coming to me so fast that I knew if I didn't stop to write it down, I would forget it. I pulled over on the side of the interstate and searched fervently for a piece of paper and a pen.

I was so frustrated that I didn't find either. I did, however, find a napkin and a lip liner. I then jotted the entire song down. Oh, how I wish I could find that scrap now! T.G. called me on the way home, and when I told him I was on the side of the road, he was worried sick. I said, "Oh, don't be worried, I'm just writing a new song." He has since learned that this is a normal occurrence for me.

The very next day, I went into the studio to record my new music. I was moved to tears to hear this song I had just written the night before come to life. I quickly made copies and gave them to Conway's children. Never in a million years did I ever think this song would go on to be heard by millions worldwide a few years later. The label wanted to release "Goodbye Darlin'" as my first single and also allowed me to film a video to coincide.

We filmed the video at Twitty City, the former home of Conway. His daughter Kathy was with me as we shot the video, and his family was kind enough to offer some never-before-seen footage for us to include. What a total joy! I seriously felt both he and my dad that evening during the filming.

"Goodbye Darlin'" Video

As a side note, I also had a new photoshoot done at my mom's home on that very day. A friend of mine was shooting pictures of me without using any flash. He only used natural light. He was shocked (and I mean seriously shocked) from his camera, enough to drop it about five frames into the session. He was later surprised to see that the photo he took had something weird on the image, as he had never seen before. It was little green orbs in a cross formation over my chest.

Only later on did I ever question what those orbs might signify in my life as my health was about to be challenged.

Note the green orbs in a cross formation.

I digress, back to my story. The record label released my song, and thanks to social media, I was able to get my music to new fans all over the world! It was almost instant! I remember getting emails from people in England, Malta, and even France, telling me how much they loved my song about Conway. Oh wow, that stranger's prayer really must have kicked in. From that point on, anytime someone says they're praying for me, I take it super seriously.

I was on fire with the excitement of the possibilities. I remember telling myself that I would never doubt God again! By the way, I have no idea who the woman was that prayed for me and have never seen her since. I consider her what I now call a *Drop-In*. I will later experience a few more of those in my life.

At this point, still just a dating partner to T.G., I would sing on a few of his shows, thanks to the song picking up interest all over the country. It was so wonderful being on stage with the love of my life and getting to share my new music with his audience. His fans were a continued branch from Conway's fans too, so they automatically seemed to enjoy this song in his honor. I was living my best life, but things were getting ready to change drastically.

Kelly's Portraits Of Her Two Favorite People - Her Mom and Dad: Velton and Nancy Lang

Scan this code with your camera-equipped smartphone to view the bonus video. (Most IOS and Android devices can read QR codes by scanning with the built-in camera.) If you do not have a QR app on your phone visit your app store and search for QR code reader.

6

THE BIG C

I don't believe in coincidences! In November of 2003, I remember sitting on the edge of my bed while the girls played on the computer in my bedroom. I was quickly channel surfing, trying to find something to watch on TV, when I was stopped in my tracks as Oprah Winfrey had a young lady on her show. She couldn't have been more than 25 years old and was pleading with women of all ages viewing the show to please stop what they were doing and do a self-breast exam. The doctors had told her that she was too young to have breast cancer, yet lo and behold, there she was, a radiant young woman with this ugly disease trying to help others understand that it can happen to us at any age.

Click, Click; I changed the channel. I was looking for something more fun to watch. I mean, who wants to see that? I could not relate to what she was talking about, I thought. Still, something kept nudging me to go back and watch that program (Oh great, that gut instinct again).

It was as if I couldn't turn away from a bad accident, so I watched her. I began, very reluctantly, I might add, to do my very first breast self-exam.

I felt my right breast, "Ahh, smooth as a baby's bottom!" Then I reached for my left side. "Oh no, what is this I feel?" It was a hard, pea-sized little knot under my armpit, probably just gristle. I also felt an egg-shaped lump below it that felt much different. Oh well, I wasn't going to worry since I had heard most women had lumpy breasts with no problems, right?

I remember running into my girlfriend Linda at a shoe store. She taught both of my girls in the first grade. She told me that she had just been diagnosed with breast cancer. I admired her smile and her spunk during such a dark time in her life. Internally I vowed that if I were ever to be dealt something that traumatic, Linda is who I wanted to be just like. I told her that day about the two lumps I'd felt a few weeks before. She urged me to get them checked out, but I didn't. God was trying to drop me hints! *DUH!* That was no coincidence that I ran into her.

The next week, I remember looking through a message board on a friend's website and came across another old friend's name. I hadn't seen her or even thought of her in years, but she mentioned that she had just bought one of my CDs just two hours earlier and that God must have laid us on each other's hearts. I didn't know why at the time, but I sure do now; these were more examples of Drop Ins. A few weeks went by after our initial visit by phone, and I got an email from her saying she had also been diagnosed with breast cancer. I thought, "Gosh, this word is popping up in my life more regularly than I'm comfortable with." She kept all of her friends posted with weekly updates about her health and progress; quite honestly, it wounded my spirit to read all of the details, like it was hitting too close to home for me, and I didn't know why. In hindsight, reconnecting with her was no coincidence either.

I decided to go to my regular OB/GYN to ease the ongoing internal nagging I kept hearing. I trusted this doctor who delivered my children. I asked for an ultrasound to check out these concerning lumps I had felt. I did that test on Monday, and I still hadn't heard the results from that test by Friday. I could have gone the rest of my life thinking, "No news is good news," but I called and asked about my results. (This was my first lesson in taking charge of my own health and being more assertive.)

The doctor said, "You look okay to me and you are too young to worry about it. We will just watch it…blah blah blah." I thought, yeah, that's what they told the girl on Oprah earlier too. I asked her why she hadn't called me as I had been on pins and needles waiting to hear the results. She told me that it wasn't their responsibility to call the patient when test results come back. She said it was the patient's responsibility to call the doctor because they get so busy that things slip through the cracks. I couldn't believe what she was saying! If I hadn't followed up, would I still be alive today? Who knows… but, the lesson I learned from that situation brought me through this new phase of my life.

I began working out at a local gym, walking on the treadmill every day. While passing the time away, I would read the magazines they had lying around. It was so weird. It seemed that every one I picked up had an article in it about breast cancer, specifically breast cancer under the age of 40! Well, I was 35, so that began to resonate louder and louder. I felt God's winking at me again and again. I chose not to worry about these subtle hints since I had already done my due diligence by having the doctor give me a *clean slate*. Besides that, I was the picture of health and had so much to look forward to. Having just signed with a new record label, I was beginning to travel and make headway with my career. T.G. and I had been dating for many years, and we had been traveling a lot. I was also set to headline my first concert in Bern, Switzerland. I didn't have time for any health concerns. I was too busy enjoying life.

Every time I'd take a shower though, I'd find myself reaching for these spots under my left arm to check if they were growing any larger, or hopefully, just maybe they would magically go away; no such luck. I knew this might be something I needed to deal with when I returned from my concert in Switzerland.

I had a lot of weird *coincidences* of so many people coming into my life with little warning signs for me to check my breasts. Some distant relatives were going through cancer battles of their own; some acquaintances had reached out to me over social media asking me if I'd ever had a mammogram. It was strange, like God was circling my life with little hints as to what was about to come.

I chose not to ask my doctor for an updated mammogram or any other tests until I returned from my trip because deep down inside, in the core of my soul, I knew these weren't just coincidences. I knew in my heart that when I got back into the United States, I had a battle ahead of me. I just knew it.

I had a blast touring Bern, Switzerland. It is absolutely gorgeous over there, and the lifelong friends that I made were priceless. Looking back at the pictures from that trip, I looked healthy, radiant and happy. Nobody would have ever imagined the inner fear that I had because I hid it with a genuine smile.

I was truly in the moment. The beauty of the Swiss Alps overwhelmed me, for in my gut, I truly knew something wasn't right. I remember consciously looking at the glory of these mountains and wondered if I'd ever see this beautiful place again. I drank it all in.

As I was grabbing my bag at the Zurich airport, a sharp pain bolted into the side of my breast, causing me to drop my luggage. I had always heard that cancer didn't hurt. Well, God had been whispering to me by sending little warning signs, and I wouldn't listen. So I guess He finally struck me with something I could feel and wouldn't be able to ignore. I didn't let my mother, who was traveling with me, know what had just happened because I didn't want to alarm her. I made a pact with myself to get this checked out when I got back.

On the plane home, I was reading a *Redbook* magazine that mentioned *diagnostic mammograms.* I didn't know there were different types before reading that article. It said that this type was more specific than a regular mammogram. I decided that I would insist on getting one when I got home. I was really beginning to worry and truthfully was looking forward to getting answers, even though I really didn't want to know if it was bad news.

Within a week, my doctor allowed me a diagnostic mammogram. Strangely enough, *NOTHING* showed up in that test. Whew! However, something told me to dig deeper. These rock-hard knots were still under my arm, and I wanted to know what they were. I then asked for them to perform an ultrasound to check these out.

The girl doing my ultrasound said that she couldn't see the spots I was concerned about on her test. I knew that it might offend her by asking her to go a little deeper with her wand, but I didn't care; this was my life we were talking about. She still didn't go to the exact spot. I took a big chance of making her mad at me, but I then asked if I could hold her ultrasound wand and push deep enough to show her what I had been feeling. Within seconds, you could visibly see her expression change. Her face dropped and turned white. She got very quiet and raced out of the room. She brought the radiologist back with her, and within minutes they were telling me that I needed to see my OBGYN asap for further details. That afternoon I was in my OBGYN's office hearing that I needed a biopsy to determine what this was; from the same doctor that claimed this was nothing seven months earlier. It makes me wonder if she had biopsied this earlier, would the cancer have spread? Would I still be alive today if I had just trusted the mammogram? Oh, so many questions.

She recommended a doctor in my own town, a dry, crusty, old-fashioned man who I felt blew me and my concerns off. He wanted to do a lumpectomy in the hospital and then test to see if it was cancer. That seemed a little barbaric to me as I was hoping for just a biopsy. He said he could only work me in after his vacation and just before Christmas weeks and weeks later. Something told me not to allow him to work on me. I questioned why they would do such an extensive surgery when a biopsy would be a less invasive approach. Truth be told, I didn't want my pretty breasts scarred up if they didn't have to be. Vanity ladies, I'm sure you get it.

I decided to shop around for a doctor that would listen to my concerns, much to his dismay. I checked with some friends asking, "Who do you recommend?" but I didn't want anyone to know it was for me. I was asking for a "Friend," LOL.

I found a doctor at Baptist Hospital; he was a funny young man. That was important to me at that time. He assured me that it was probably nothing, but yes, they could do a simple biopsy, adding that I was very smart to think things through before I just let anyone cut me open. Whew ~ I was relieved and felt smart and powerful. That was another step on my ladder of knowledge that I began climbing. This small decision gave me the confidence to be proactive in asking more questions and the courage to say no if I wasn't comfortable.

My older sister Traci happened to be in town for her annual visit from Arizona. Looking back, it seems awfully strange that she always happens to be in town when something big happens in our family - good or bad; the births of our babies, weddings, the death of our father, and now this biopsy. For some reason, it scared me that she was here for this test. I looked at it as a sign that God knew that I might need her here for comfort. Unfortunately, I was correct.

Traci Stengel (sister) and Kelly

She took me to the Baptist Hospital, where I went into this office. I was scared but fascinated by all of the pamphlets and booklets on breast cancer. I remember thinking, "I should grab some of those on how to talk to children about cancer," but I also thought that if I brought them home, it would make that become a reality, so I left them there.

They called me back into a sterile room. When I get nervous, I tend to laugh, and I make jokes. I was *VERY* giddy on this day. For the life of me, I cannot understand why I wasn't offered a Valium to calm me down. They said, "This won't hurt," then *POW*, like a staple gun, ten times into my left breast, with nothing to numb the area at all, this instrument went in and out of me, pulling more tissue each time it left my breast. I could feel a tugging. I kept visualizing the cancer (if it indeed was that) being drug across my healthy tissue and wondered if there might be some concern about that.

No one seemed concerned at all; they put a little metal marker in place of the tumor that had been biopsied. Because it appeared to be so little on ultrasound, the doctor wanted to have a place to refer back to later. I was relieved by that remark thinking maybe she had removed it all and that I may be one and done with this whole process at that moment. Boy, was I wrong. I was assured that 80% of all biopsies turn out to be nothing. That was a nice reassurance, but I would have appreciated a Valium too.

I asked when I would get my results back but honestly found myself not really wanting to know; how immature of me. They told me that I could possibly hear within the next two days. I knew Traci's plane was scheduled for the next day, but I asked her to postpone leaving. If she could stay just one more day, it would also allow her to go to a birthday lunch for our brother Scott on December 15. I loved that lunch. Looking back, that was the last time I felt normal.

The week before, I had been on a television show called *Country Request Live* on Great American Country. I got to sing a song that I had written a few months earlier called "I'm Not Going Anywhere." I received a lot of compliments saying how healthy I looked, how nice and trim, and how my complexion was radiant. I took that as a hopeful sign that everything would turn out okay and that I had nothing to worry about.

I was asked to sing at a party that night to fill in for a girl who couldn't make it. Singing was, and always has been, cathartic for me. So I agreed to sing even though I was nervous about the pending news. It helped me pass the time and get my mind off of the results.

The next day, Traci, my mom, and I went Christmas shopping. I called the doctor's office a few times throughout the day to see if they had read the results. The nurse told me that the doctor was still in surgery and he would call me the moment he could. I told her that my sister was postponing her trip until I heard the results, and if he could expedite his reading of the tests, that would be so helpful. I think that really sped things up a bit.

We drove to Marshall's, and I ran into my art teacher Joyce. She asked me about my biopsy. She had breast cancer years before and had been concerned for me. It was no coincidence that I was standing next to this cancer survivor when my doctor called.

"Miss Lang? Dr. Lynch, I know you're anxious to get these results" "Yes," I said calmly, as I put a pair of boots I was buying for my daughter Payton in the cart. "Are you with family?" he asked. *OH GOD, OH NO!* So this is what it feels like to get this kind of news! My heart started pounding, and I got very lightheaded. It seemed like I was in a bad movie.

At first, he didn't want to tell me the results and asked that I come to his office first thing in the morning. I begged him to just tell me then. I didn't want to wait any longer, and I needed to know so Traci could stay in town another day if I needed her. He asked if I could find a place to sit down as he told me the dreaded news, so right there, between the junior section and sportswear, I learned my fate.

He said, "okay, I have good news and bad news; the large mass in your breast, the egg-shaped one, is not cancer. It is a form of pre-cancer, but if left in there long enough, it could be really bad. It is called PASH. The other tumor is breast cancer, and we need to meet as soon as we can tomorrow to discuss your options." I reluctantly agreed. I asked if we could make it around 10:00 am, and he said, "No Ma'am, I need to see you at 8:00 am."

His urgency to see me so quickly let me know I was in a bit of danger, so I was instantly terrified. I sat down and began to tremble. Mom, Traci, and Joyce all held me. My friend Brenda was there too. Ironically, she had just been telling me before my doctor had called that her recent mammogram came back clear and that I probably had nothing to worry about. I often wonder how she must have felt after she heard my news.

I guess I was in a state of shock for some time because I felt the dire need to finish shopping that day. I had a lot to get done before Christmas if I was going to be having surgery. I was still in a power search for a bicycle for Payton. Cancer or no cancer, I was on a mission. Looking back, that attitude carried me through this battle. I didn't have time for this crap.

I called T.G. right away. He was living in Memphis at the time, working with his family in a company called Faith (they made hip and knee replacements). Memphis is a solid 3 ½ hour drive from Hendersonville. He must have driven at warp speed to get home to me because he made the trip in 2 hours and 45 min, but it seemed like an eternity. I later asked him how he felt when I told him the news. He was broken-hearted. He told me that he cried and prayed all the way to Hendersonville. I couldn't wait to just curl up in his strong arms and cry.

On December 16, 2004, at 8:00 am sharp, mom, Traci, T.G., and I were at the doctor's office waiting to hear my fate. I was trembling inside, literally shaking with hard rigors. Everyone tried to comfort me, telling me it would be okay, but none of us honestly believed that.

In came this charming and handsome doctor who proceeded to tell me about the biopsy and what his plan would be if I were his wife. He wanted me to get a double mastectomy asap and had already scheduled me with a plastic surgeon to handle the deed. I could see his mouth moving, but I didn't comprehend a thing he was saying. I was so grateful that my sister had brought a notepad with her to jot down everything he was saying, or I certainly would have forgotten half of it. I recommend to anyone going to a doctor's office that you use the voice recorder on your phone to record the conversation to avoid mis-understanding any important information.

I was mortified! I mean, the tumors were tiny and only on my left side...couldn't we compromise here and only do a lumpectomy on that area? He proceeded to tell me that since I was so young, the statistics show that they needed to be a bit more aggressive since most of these types of cancers can move to the other side. I was astounded by this news as I was rather fond of my breasts. I had implants done several years earlier, and I was so sad at the thought of having them removed completely. I didn't feel like this male doctor really understood what that might feel like to a woman. It is such an integral part of a woman's femininity.

I could feel my rage taking over as I began to rebut his decision. "Now, hold on a minute," I said. (Children, cover your ears here, for I'm about to say something a bit distasteful and completely unladylike, sorry.) I asked this doctor, "If you had a tiny little cancer spot on your belly button, would you let them take off your penis and your balls?" He began coughing and stammering and then excused himself from the room immediately. I heard him giggle outside of the door, but I wasn't joking at all. I was in this doctor's office for 45 minutes total, but it seemed like an eternity.

One of the harshest lessons that I learned was that later when I received an explanation of benefits from the insurance company regarding this office visit, I realized that I had been charged with two separate visits. When I called the office to ask about this obvious mistake, they proceeded to tell me that since I was in there for longer than 30 minutes, they were legally allowed to charge me for two office visits. WOW! I didn't know I was on a clock to get this life-shattering news. After that, I was cautious of everything and everyone, assuming that it was turning into a money game. So sad.

I went to his obligatory plastic surgeon's appointment, but I refused to even look at the books of reconstructed breasts. I'm sure this doctor was amazing, but I just couldn't do it. There had to be another way.

The doctor told me that I needed to go to Tennessee Oncology to meet my new oncologist. I had no idea what an oncologist was at the time, and now I have my very own? Oh wow!

I met with her, and she recommended a female surgeon named Dr. Laura Lawson to talk about my hope to have a lumpectomy. She was so awesome and understanding. I received some great advice during this visit. She told me they could tell who would or would not survive just by whether or not the patient had a good and positive attitude when they walked in the door; versus a poor and bitter one. I chose that very day to try to be positive, even if it meant faking a smile. I didn't want to tempt fate. Until then, I didn't realize how much mental attitude could affect healing. I quickly learned that we truly are Mind, Body, and Spirit.

Around this time, I felt that it might be time for me to talk to my daughters about the impending future that lay ahead. What do you say to a nine and thirteen-year-old;

how do I begin? You better sit down, kids? I felt that I had to be completely honest and shoot straight with them.

Payton, my oldest, got home a little earlier than Kennedy, so I decided to tell her first. Actually, they are both very intuitive girls, and she could tell something was wrong with me the second she came in from school. I told her that I had some tests done, and it showed up as breast cancer. She just stood there looking stunned, almost as if she hadn't really heard me. I guess that is a lot for a thirteen-year-old girl to swallow. Big tears welled up in her eyes, and she began to hug me tightly. She asked me if I would lose my hair, but at the time, I wasn't entirely sure if that would be the case. She then offered me her long beautiful brown hair as a gift if I ever needed it. That was the most precious gesture I could ever imagine. What a beautiful and generous heart she has. I hoped that it would never come to that, but I thanked her.

When Kennedy got home, I told her. Maybe it was her age, but she just changed the subject very quickly. She didn't want to be bothered with this interrupting her playtime. I was a little hurt by her avoidance, but I realized that maybe that was her unique way of dealing with it.

I noticed that anytime someone would ask me how I was feeling, she seemed annoyed, as if we ignored the cancer, maybe it would just go away. I noticed that it might be starting to bother her internally, though. Her grades began to drop immediately, and she couldn't seem to shake her head cold, thus causing her to miss more school and therefore worsen her grades even further. During treatments, I had to rely on my mom, my ex, and his mother to help get them to and from school and doctor's appointments.

My mom asked Kennedy if maybe she thought the reason she was sick so often was that she might be worried about me, explaining that sometimes when we worry, we can make ourselves sick. She said, "No, I'm just not feeling well." Mom insisted, "Kennedy, mamma is very sick. Are you afraid? You may be run down from fear and can't kick this constant sinus infection." Kennedy insisted, "No, I'm just not feeling well; this has nothing to do with mamma." Mom kept on, "Yeah, but Kennedy..." Kennedy just stopped her in her tracks. "Look Nanny, mom said not to worry about her, so I'm not! I am just sick!" Funny, I told her to make up her bed and clean her room, but she never listened to me on that!

Kelly and her daughter Kennedy

A few weeks after my diagnosis, Kennedy came home from school, asking why everyone was being *so nice* to her. Complete strangers offered to help her and take her places, always asking how her mom was feeling. I smiled and said, "What do you tell them?" She said, "I tell them you're fine; you've got me don't you?"

We all went to a Relay For Life event during that time, held at the track of my previous high school. My sweet mother brought a candle in honor of me, and it glowed with my name on it in the dark. But I remember glowing even more when I saw Payton gather several friends around her that night and prayed out loud unashamedly for her mother. I have wonderful daughters. I hope to make them proud of my courage as they one day read this book.

Kelly and her daughter Payton

Several months later, I began to feel very uncomfortable in my lower stomach and decided to check it out. My doctor told me that since I wasn't planning on having any more children, I should consider a hysterectomy. Based upon the scans, she had feared that there might be some cancer activity showing up in my female area. I was more than ready to get that done as it was causing me such pain. So, just a few months after my chemo and radiation were complete, a hysterectomy was scheduled. About four months after my hysterectomy that my oncologist had ordered, I went in for my yearly check-up with her. To my disgust, she had the nerve to ask me how my periods were. Since I had been her patient for so long, I was in total disbelief that she had forgotten that she had ordered the hysterectomy. Was she actually reading my chart? Was I just a number to her? I had been told that my cancer was estrogen positive so, I was a little confused that the surgeon kept trying to encourage me to keep just one ovary in. I didn't want to take a chance of having ovarian cancer in my future and just opted to remove them both. The doctor tried to warn me of how difficult it would be after the surgery since it automatically puts a woman into menopause. Since I was a cancer patient, they couldn't allow me any support of hormones. I felt confident that I'd be okay since the chemo had already put me into premature menopause before, and I had done well. Of course, that was just a small period of time that I was without my regular period. A few night sweats and feeling horrible for a few months wasn't the worst thing that I had gone through, but that was only on a temporary basis. Now, this was going to be a permanent thing. *OH WOW!* No one could have warned me how bad it was going to be.

The doctor also put me on a drug called Tamoxifen at the time, which I was supposed to be on for five years to block the estrogen. I immediately gained 15lbs, and my body began to ache. It was horrible. I was really starting to slip into depression. I went into severe panic mode and decided very quickly that this drug was not my friend. I can not recommend this to anyone else, but I got off it very quickly against the advice of my doctors; this was no way of life for me.

For five long, moody, and sweaty years, I stayed away from any hormone help. Experts told me that if I wanted to consider any alternative hormones, I'd at least have to be five years out before any doctor would even talk to me. I was very blessed to find New Life's Physicians. They did a panel of bloodwork on me. The sweet nurse actually had tears in her eyes when she read me the results. She asked how I even had the strength to walk into her office as my numbers had been so cripplingly low. I excitedly but fearfully allowed them to implant bioidentical hormones into my hip. The way this process works is, once the pellets are implanted into the skin, the blood flows over them, releasing a small amount into the bloodstream daily. Within a week, I noticed the night sweats diminish. I felt more alive and clearer with better muscle tone within two weeks. By the next month, I felt better than I had in years. I had to make a decision. However many years I may have to live on this earth, I want quality of life over quantity.

The doctors carefully balance the amount of estrogen, progesterone, and testosterone within the body, restoring the patient back to a time when their bodies were younger. Sign me up!

I was doing so well; I talked T.G. into getting his hormones checked out. He too was noticing that age was taking a toll on him. Again, within weeks, he saw a dramatic improvement in all areas. We are so grateful for this process in our lives, and we highly recommend it to all of our friends.

Scan this code with your camera-equipped smartphone to view the bonus video. (Most IOS and Android devices can read QR codes by scanning with the built-in camera) If you do not have a QR app on your phone visit your app store and search for QR code reader.

SCAN ME

7

I'M NOT GOING ANYWHERE (THE SONG)

A few months before my diagnosis, I was witness to a friend watching her husband going through a medical crisis. He had hospice workers all around him, but he only seemed comforted when his wife would tell him, "Honey, I'm right here, I'm not leaving you, I'm not going anywhere." How comforting, I thought. Wow, if I am ever sick like that, I'd hoped to have someone say those exact words to me. Be careful what you wish for.

After seeing her comfort him with those kind words, I began to hear a beautiful melody in my head. I wrote an instrumental on a keyboard that T.G. had gotten me for Christmas the previous year. I told him that the title was "I'm Not Going Anywhere." He laughed and said, "Where are the words?" I was trying to be cool and just replied that I only heard this as a lovely instrumental, when in all honesty, I might have been too lazy to write any lyrics. Or....maybe the words would be too painful if I had written down what was in my subconscious.

As always, T.G. encouraged me to stretch a bit more out of my comfort zone. I was challenged to go to the keyboard again and again until the lyrics came to me.

Take my hand, don't let go
Look in my eyes, and in my soul
Hold me close, hold me near
Please let go, of all your fear...I'm Not Going Anywhere.

These are the lyrics I started with. A tear came to T.G.'s eye when I sang them to him with the melody I had already created. He said it was beautiful and encouraged me to finish it. I felt that it was special as I had gotten emotional myself when I wrote it. I went back to writing more lyrics...

Seasons change with the wind
But I'll be here till the end
Friends may come and then they go
But there's one thing you should know
I'm Not Going Anywhere.
I'd give my heart to you if your's stopped beating
Part your lips with mine if you weren't breathing
You have no burden that I wouldn't bear
I'm Not Going Anywhere
I'll still be here when you close your eyes
There's no place I'd rather be
Than here by your side.

I cried like a baby at my piano as these words resonated within me. I had no idea as to why at the time, but I would understand later.

I went into the studio soon after and recorded it. This song landed on my album *11:11*. I love when I complete a song, record it, and it sounds like it did in my head once it is finished. As a songwriter, if I have a song stirring in my mind and I am not able to record it, it is like clothes scattered all over the floor that are not hung properly; a jumbled mess in my head that needs to be complete in order for my mind to rest.

As I was going through breast cancer treatments, I lost my long hair after three weeks. The doctor told me it would be exactly 21 days, and it was. I lost my eyebrows and lashes too. It's just a shame it didn't take those tiny little chin hairs along with it, dang it. I covered my bald head and drew in my brows as much as I could, never letting anyone see this side of me, especially T.G.

One day, after taking my daughters to school, I decided to shower and then really look at myself in the mirror, scars, bald head, green complexion, and all. Oh my gosh, I looked like a monster! I began to wail, not cry. It was a moan from deep inside so agonizing I began to frighten myself. I was startled when T.G. walked into the bathroom. He had let himself in with his key and ran upstairs to see what this horrible noise was. I think it freaked him out to see me this way. He immediately wrapped me in my white terry cloth robe and pulled me down onto his lap near my walk-in closet. He rocked me in his arms and kept drying my tears. I was so embarrassed for him to see me this way and told him that this was his perfect way out. He wasn't obligated at this time to stay with me as we were only dating and that he should go now.

I honestly felt that since he couldn't commit to me before this, why on earth would he want to stick around? I begged him to stop looking at me as I was so gross and was probably not going to survive. You know what he told me? Over and Over? He said, "Kel, I love you. You're the most beautiful and strong woman I've ever known, and *I'm not going anywhere*." WOW! My words that I had written just months before came full circle. I can truthfully say, at that very moment, I truly believed him. It was the most pivotal moment in our lives. No marriage license was any stronger than that bond.

T.G. was incredible throughout the entire experience, taking me to all of my chemo and radiation appointments. He even sat with me during dreaded MRIs and held my hand as it stuck out of the big scary machine. He knows how claustrophobic I am, so he would sing to me as I lay frightened in each one. God, I love this man.

I am completely aware of the stats of how many partners don't tend to stick around during such a crisis, and I thank God every day for his commitment. I wish that all men could take a page out of T.G. Sheppard's handbook on how to help your partner get through such dark times. He's the best of the best. I know how blessed I am, trust me.

Years later, I was thrilled when T.G. and Crystal Gayle (one of my musical heroes) recorded my song "I'm Not Going Anywhere" on his duets album, *Partners In Rhyme*, which was later released as *Legendary Friends and Country Duets*. This song also landed in one of Burt Reynold's last movies, called *The Deal*. It was so exciting to attend the premiere in Las Vegas and walk the red carpet for that event. It's a good movie; y'all should check it out.

As a songwriter, it is highly unusual to get a song heard, cut, or placed in any way. I knew this song was different than anything I'd ever written, but I had no idea what lie ahead. I want to take this time to encourage anyone out there that is creative in any way. Remember, nothing is created in vain. If God gave you the idea to create something, He has a reason for doing so. We might not ever understand why, but just do it anyway. His timing is not our timing. I had no idea that something I would have written 16 years before would be used in a national commercial and be helpful for so many, but God did.

As I was going through chemotherapy treatments, I would walk every day at the YMCA with friend and country star, Lorrie Morgan and we started talking about music one day. I had begun writing with her piano player and told her about some music ideas we had come up with. At the time, she had only known me as a singer but never a writer. I was rather shy about showing that side of my talent because it's like bearing a secret part of your soul when you share what you've written. She was a huge musical influence on me, and I wasn't sure if she would think I was a good writer. I reluctantly shared "I'm Not Going Anywhere" with her, and she *LOVED* it. So much so, she wanted to play it at her son Jesse Keith's graduation party. Her appreciation for my writing led us to write her entire album, *I Walk Alone*. Putting her life story to music was an incredible time for us both. We had such a wonderful time creating beautiful music together.

A little-known fact about mine and Lorrie's longtime friendship: years before, I was working singing on *The Ralph Emery Show* and had just filled Lorrie's spot that she had sung on before her career skyrocketed. I was working at Dillards in Rivergate Mall selling fragrances when she came to my counter. I was so embarrassed. I didn't really know her well at the time, and I didn't want her to see me having to work outside of the music business, but I'm sure glad she did.

I helped her with her purchase and shot the breeze with her while trying to look calm. She said, "How's your music career coming along?" I was so embarrassed. I said, "Well, if it was doing so great, I wouldn't be working here, would I?" We both laughed.

She asked if I had any music recorded that she could listen to. I had made a little recording on a tape. I mailed it to her. She called me a few days later from the road and said she loved it and wanted to help me. She and I picked out some great songs together, and she took me into the studio with her producer Richard Landis and made a demo. I was so excited and nervous. I didn't want to let her down. She also took it a step further. She had been getting her beautiful infamous short blonde hair done by a world-renown hairdresser from Australia. This stylist was only in town a few times a year. She would set up her pop-up shop in the Spence Manor in downtown Nashville. She did all of the top stars' hair, and her price proved her importance. Lorrie paid for me to get my hair and makeup done by her before I was to perform on *The Statler Brothers Show*. How nice was that? I wish more artists helped others as she did me.

Kelly and Lorrie Morgan

She also paid for me to have makeup and hair and an incredible photoshoot at her home. LORD!, what a funny story that ended up being!

Lorrie's bedroom had gorgeous white carpet. Her home had a country flare but was super glamorous. I was so nervous being there. I'm like a bull in a china shop and didn't want to break anything that I couldn't afford to fix. Earlier that day, before the shoot, I had put a temporary rinse on my hair to darken it. I had no idea that the photographer wanted me to have *The Wet* hair look in my pics. I honestly didn't think a thing about it. The shoot was in a barn on her property. All went well until Lorrie came out from her bedroom with a bewildered look on her face. "Kel? Do you have a color on your hair?" I said, "Yes, why do you ask?" She proceeded to tell me that my hair dye had dripped all through her white carpet in her bedroom! I was horrified! When something like that happens to me, I totally have *NO* idea what to do to fix it! I have zero cleaning skills. What was I to do? I have been mortified to this day, but we have been friends so long that time revealed how she was to get me back by accident.

Lorrie knew how much I loved SeaWorld and offered to take me along with her when she performed. Oh, how I loved her glam bus. It was gorgeous and feminine, just like her. She offered me a glass of wine in one of her monogrammed glasses with L.M. perfectly etched into each one. They reeked with class. I poured myself a glass, and when I was done, I put it into the sink; then the bus shifted, causing my glass to shatter. *OH CRAP!* I was shocked! I just stared at the broken glass, hoping that it hadn't happened. I didn't even try to pick it up, frozen like a deer in headlights! I'm sure she thought, "Clean up after yourself!" but she just laughed. I offered to buy her another, but she said they couldn't be recreated anymore. How embarrassing!

I was surprised that she invited me back on the bus a week or so later to go to another show of hers. I always try to turn awkward situations into comedy skits to take the sting out of it. I decided to buy a plastic wine glass, you know, the kind where the stem screws off of the bottom?

I wrote K.L. on the side of the plastic glass with a sharpie and hung it upside down in her wine glass holder. We both had a nice chuckle about it.

Imagine my surprise, when many, many years later, at my 50th birthday party, she gifted me the same plastic wine glass with my *K.L.* initials on it from years before. So funny! I was shocked she'd kept it all this time.

The plastic KL wineglass

I loved it when years later, at mine and T.G.'s annual Christmas party, Lorrie accidentally spilled an entire glass of red wine onto our sofa and ivory carpet. Again, I was paralyzed and just stared at her trying to clean up the mess. She was asking for Oxi Clean or anything to get wine stains out of the carpet. I had nothing! She got on the floor and ferociously blotted the stains up. I just laughed, knowing it would eventually come up. She was freaked out! Later that night, one of T.G.'s band members who happened to be at the party called to thank us for the invite. He said, "T, that party was very fun and so special! The food was nice, and probably expensive, what like, $1,000? And the drinks, maybe $1,500? But Lorrie Morgan on her hands and knees cleaning red wine off of the carpet was priceless!"

We got a huge laugh out of that. The wine came up, and the friendship continues to this day. Very much like the lyrics of my song, "Friends may come and then they go," although many months may pass as to when Lorrie and I can see each other, we both know when it comes to my love and appreciation for her, I'm not going anywhere.

I was later amazed when this song, "I'm Not Going Anywhere," that I wrote so long ago, would reappear in a big way and change my life. I can't wait to share more about this song in just a bit.

Scan this code with your camera-equipped smartphone to view the bonus video. (Most IOS and Android devices can read QR codes by scanning with the built-in camera.) If you do not have a QR app on your phone visit your app store and search for QR code reader.

8

SURGERY DAY

My breast surgeon, Dr. Laura Lawson, is a quiet, serious, and compassionate doctor, but my favorite thing about her is that she is the biggest Elvis fan! Once she realized that T.G. had been friends with Elvis and had even lived at Graceland, it blew her mind. I always got tickled when she talked to him about her love of The King while examining my poor breasts. I just adored her and still consider her a dear friend.

Being a female, I think she better understood my concerns to keep my breasts intact. I appreciated that she allowed me to negotiate my options to leave my implants in and just try for a lumpectomy, so a lumpectomy we did.

She told me that it was good that I did my research and was proactive to ask hard questions because facts were adding up that a lumpectomy was seemingly just as successful as mastectomies had been. She did warn me that I would have to do at least six weeks of radiation afterward. I was okay with all of that. I felt that it was a good compromise.

On Jan 4, 2005, I showed up at the hospital, ready to get this behind me. The receptionist immediately asked me for my insurance card and $500.00. It was so weird writing a check to have something you don't want to have done to you. I wish it had been a tummy tuck or lipo; at least that would have been a fun improvement. I was wheeled down to a terribly cold room for the procedure. They would locate the exact spot of my tumors by stabbing sharp needles into my nipple and into the hard knots under my arm. All the while, the numbing cream had worn off hours before, and I was awake this whole time! They then made me do several MRI and ultrasound images while the long needles protruded from my breast. It was brutal, just barbaric. I remember calling Jesus's name out loud and begging Him to make them stop. Still to this day, I will say that is the most painful thing I've ever experienced. I think they now anesthetize people due to my crying like a little girl so loudly. When I returned to my room before surgery, I recall begging them to sedate me to get me out of this agony.

On the way to surgery, T.G. and mom held my hand until the doctors made them leave my side. The only thing I remember is how cold this room was, and the lights were so very bright. Being medicated, time obviously went fast for me, but mom and T.G. said it was the longest day of their lives. I was terribly nauseous after the surgery, so the sweet nurses gave me a shot to help. It was so painful; I think I'd just have rather thrown up instead. I went home to my mother's to recover and awaited the results, hoping they had gotten it all and had clear margins.

Mom lived in a beautiful three-bedroom home in Hendersonville. I decided to stay with her during this difficult time until I recovered, and T.G. stayed in her guest room. They were so kind to help me with the girls while there. We had all of our meals together that friends from church brought by. Some of the sweetest memories were during those days.

I then received a phone call from my oncologist saying although they seemed to have gotten all of the tumors removed, they unfortunately found it within my lymph nodes. They removed a total of six, but it had been present in two. Sadly, this would now be considered *STAGE II* breast cancer, requiring me to not only have to do radiation, but now, the dreaded *CHEMO*. I bawled so hard. That was the worst news I had heard yet. I was devastated. Due to my age, they wanted to treat this very aggressively, and I was to begin right away.

My brothers came over to my mom's that evening to comfort me and discuss my dim future. My oldest brother Scott, a brain cancer survivor himself, was taking this news very hard, but in his usual witty way, he did change the dark mood when someone called the house. He was trying to comfort me and yet still be light-hearted at the same time. As he answered the call, he said in a sad voice, "Can't ya see we are grieving over here?" Then he pushed the answer button, and in a jovial voice he said "Hello!" We all cracked up. I love that my entire family has such a great sense of humor. That witty, self-deprecating attitude kept me laughing through the entire otherwise solemn event.

As a few days went by, the idea of having to go through chemo was sinking in, and then, I got another blow. While I was driving through town, I got a call on my cell phone from my oncologist with some grave news. In her defense, she wanted me to come into the office to hear what she had to say; but at that point, I asked her to please just tell me right then and there. She said, "Kelly, I suspect this cancer is much worse than we originally thought. I don't think that your cancer is coming from the breast. I worry that it may be coming from another organ like the liver or spleen, and we need to do more tests to check this out further." I asked, "Wouldn't you just treat it with the same chemo you had already planned if that was indeed the case?" She said, "No, all we can do at this point is just make you comfortable."

I almost wrecked my car. I began to shake so terribly, asking her why she felt this way, but I trusted her judgment. I agreed to do more tests and then meet her that Friday morning for my results. My only hope was *PRAYER*. I immediately remembered that the night before my surgery, Jan 3, 2005, my friend Darla and two of her prayer warrior friends came over to my modest condo to pray for me.

They laid hands on me and began to rub oil on my forehead. They started speaking in foreign languages, which I later understood to be speaking in tongues. I was fascinated. They prayed that God would work a miracle in my life and that the cancer cells would line up and march out of my body and that the doctors would shake their heads in amazement and disbelief that all of the cancer would be gone. They claimed that the doctors would declare that it was a miracle.

I have to admit that my faith was beginning to waver. None of that prayer seemed reasonable at that point, but I had learned my lesson from before and just appreciated the fact that anyone would pray for me.

I had another Catholic friend give me Holy Water and Holy Oil to use before having a PET scan done that week to determine my fate. I am not Catholic, so I was not really aware of how to use these precious tools, but I totally appreciated the gifts. I was desperate to be healed, so I rubbed all of the oil all over my body and then poured the water over me afterward. I never even thought about how stupid that was until I saw the water repelling off of the oil, but hey, God knew my intentions.

I prayed a long consistent prayer during the duration of the PET scan, asking that He would allow me to see my daughters grow up. I remember wearing tiny little angel earrings they had given me to every doctor's visit or scan, and that test was no different. I lightly rubbed the little wings on them all during my prayer. They comforted me.

My mind was all over the map during the 45-minute test. I went from planning my future to planning my funeral on that cold table. I was thinking about what songs I might want to have playing at my service and wondered who would speak? Needless to say, I was scared to death. They had given me an IV to push dye into my veins to show any *Hot Spots* of cancer during the scan.

I wondered how lit up I was? I had always been told I had a bright personality, but that was one day that I was hoping to dim it down a bit.

The next day, I was sitting in the oncologist's office with T.G. and mom, awaiting the results of the tests from the day before. I knew it could go either way. I could be dying, or I could be getting great news. All of our hearts were pounding. It was eerily quiet in that tiny room that day. Every time we would hear footsteps outside in the hallway, we shook even harder. I was shaking from within. My teeth were even chattering. I wasn't cold, but just severely stressed in my bones. I began to say, "Jesus, Jesus, you are the Great Physician. Please come help me." I kid you not; the room got very blurry, almost spinning. I felt a warm flush come over me like a heated blanket, and I felt His peace beyond understanding, just like He promises us in the Bible! Friends, *GOD HIMSELF HUGGED ME THAT DAY!*

I felt His arms around me, anchoring me on that exam table, and I immediately felt calm. I have never felt anything like this before and have never experienced it since. We waited for a little over an hour there, and then we heard the clicking of my doctor's high heels coming closer to the door. Finally, she opened the door, shaking her head in disbelief as she looked over my scans. She admitted being shocked to see that my scans were completely clear of any cancer within my entire body. She said that she had no explanation for this, but I sure did! I knew God was in that room with me that day, and I knew that He had healed me. He just had to bring me to this point for me to be able to acknowledge His mighty presence. I was trembling with excitement and couldn't wait to share this miracle with the doctor. I was immediately and sadly aware that she didn't seem to be impressed with my God and His healing, but I certainly was.

She brought my spirit down quickly with her doom and gloom approach to her plan for my upcoming chemotherapy. She warned me that they would be very aggressive and assured me that I would lose my hair within 21 days.

I was scheduled for a port to be surgically implanted into my upper right chest to give the chemo directly into there instead of having an IV done each time. My veins were already so tiny, and this was the easiest way to push their meds into me. The port would prove to be much harder on my body than I thought. Unfortunately, it was implanted on top of a nerve and caused me tons of pain while it remained inside. Eventually, the port was removed but has left a scar looking like an actual small pink ribbon on my chest. How appropriate.

Before chemotherapy would begin, I received a phone call from a friend. He had started working at a new facility that was doing some very groundbreaking testing for cancer patients. He told me to ask the oncologist for a sample of my tumor so his new company could test it against several different types of chemo to decide which one it would be most receptive to. It was going to be entirely free for me!

I thought that this was a fantastic idea! It would take the guesswork completely out of it. I have never understood why they would blast the same treatment to everyone if everyone's cancer is different. My doctor refused to send my sample and told me that would never happen as long as I was in her care. I was furious at her and felt like she didn't really have her patients' care in her best interest. I felt that it was just a money game, so I began to figure out how to get through this as quickly as possible.

Scan this code with your camera-equipped smartphone to view the bonus video. (Most IOS and Android devices can read QR codes by scanning with the built-in camera) If you do not have a QR app on your phone visit your app store and search for QR code reader.

9

CHEMO

Chemotherapy began on January 26, 2005. I was to have a treatment every other week for eight weeks. The fear of chemo is actually worse than the experience itself. I was brought into a private room to receive my first round, a concoction of both Adriamycin and Cytoxan. They seemed to be the drugs of choice, not my choice, no doubt. I recall bringing my own pillow and a heated throw, and I was so glad I did. I was cold the entire time. I recommend that anyone going through this kind of treatment do the same.

Adriamycin, otherwise known as the *Red Devil* because of its bright red color in the bag, scared me the most. It actually made me pee red for a few days after. I was super frightened by it's name, and also knowing that it was not only killing my bad cells, but my good ones as well. I was told to look at this in a different light. Don't fear this day, a friend said. Choose to look at it as the Blood Of Jesus flowing through your veins, and that's exactly what I did. That small tweak in my mindset changed the entire course of my treatment. That thought was very comforting to me from then on.

Mom and T.G. sat with me through my first treatment. It wasn't as bad as I had initially thought it would be. Afterward, I went home, ate dinner, then got up the next morning thinking that I would look awful or be sick. To my amazement, I was still very healthy-looking. Rather radiant, to be exact. I didn't realize that the steroids they had given me would make me appear to have a nice sun-kissed redness to my face. It also made me feel hyper and energetic. I felt great...until 4:30 PM. Oh my goodness, it came on me like a freight train.

I crawled into mom's guest room bed, pulled the covers over my head, and don't remember much afterward. I do remember my Shih Tzu, Hannah would lay on my chest watching me breathe until I woke up. She refused to leave my side and wouldn't eat or even go potty. I also remember praying for God to either spare me of this or let me die. I remember bits and pieces of the next two or three days. It was like a very bad flu. I had to be fed, given my pills, and sometimes even be taken to the bathroom. I am not going to lie; it was awful. I was so grateful for the TV that mom had in her room during those dark days. However, I never realized how many hair commercials ran in a single day. All of these gorgeous models with their long, flowing hair was a new threat to my ego. My long, beautiful hair was soon going to be history. I hated them all.

After a few days, the fog began to lift. I woke up, and I realized I didn't feel as nauseous for the first time in days. Speaking of nausea, the meds that I was prescribed to get rid of nausea were horrible. They made me exhausted and honestly never really cut it. I had a girlfriend call me and suggest that I have someone pick up travel bands in the pharmacy for motion sickness. She had said it was the only thing that helped her with her brutal nausea during her pregnancy. They were amazing! I tell everyone I know to run, don't walk, and buy yourself some of them before their treatment ever begins. I didn't know if it was just a mind-over-matter thing as they are just little cloth bands with plastic bumps on them that squeeze your wrists. The directions say clearly to make sure and wear one on each arm, and it may or may not help everyone. They somehow work as an acupressure point. One day, I put them on and took a nap. Somehow during my rest, one of the bands had accidentally slipped off my wrist. I woke up feeling the urge to throw up instantly! I quickly realized that only one was on my wrist. I hurriedly put the other one on, and the nausea went away as fast as it had come on me.

There was also a weird metal taste in my mouth. There was really no getting around that with anything. I had burning open sores in my mouth from the chemo that only time would heal.

After a few days of constant sleeping and being so sick and weak, I could walk into the den and breathe fresh air again. Oh, Thank God! He didn't listen to my prayer to let me die!

I asked the doctor, "why do I feel like I am dying right after treatment?" and her answer really shocked me. She told me they try to bring the patient as close to death as possible without actually killing them. Wow, that's comforting!

I took the next few treatments in a more public area, surrounded by people seemingly much worse off than myself. Although I felt grateful to be less sick than them, I also felt genuinely guilty. It made me very frightened to be in that room. I still, to this day, avoid chemo rooms like the plague when I go for annual check-ups.

After each chemo round, I had to go back to the doctor the next day to have a powerful shot called Neulasta. It was to help keep my white blood cell count up. The nurse only gave me half of the dose to see if it would be enough for my body. She told me that it would also be less painful than if I took the full amount. I was grateful, less pain, and naively I thought that it would also cost half the price. Man, was I wrong! When I got the explanation of benefits from the insurance company, I was shocked that not only was I charged the full amount, but that this drug cost nearly $5,000 a shot! They had to throw away the unused portion. That sounded like a rip-off to me. I strongly feel that something should be done to regulate things like this from continuing to happen. As I was on such a tight budget as a single mother, I began to freak out each time I felt overcharged. I found myself worrying more about how on earth I would be able to pay for this than I was about trying to heal.

During my treatment, kind people from all over sent me books about cancer to read. I feel that I was given one particular book to guide my decision regarding my cancer treatment plan. It was a book called *Getting Better,*

Not Bitter by Brenda Ladun. Brenda is a newscaster in Alabama who had gone through breast cancer. She and I talked a few times over the phone, and I had read her wonderful and informative book. We had both been told that eight treatments were typical in younger patients; four of Adriamycin/Cytoxan and then four of Taxol. I had already read about the horrible side effects of Taxol, so I was concerned about taking it.

I read that Grammy-winning singer and breast cancer survivor Melissa Ethridge had appeared in an interview stating that it had begun to make her fingers go numb, causing her to quit her chemo treatment early. *ARE YOU KIDDING ME?!* I didn't realize you could just *quit* chemo. I thought I had no choice but to take all eight of the treatments because that's what my doctor said! In Brenda's book, she quit before Taxol too! Her doctor told her that it would only be a 1% benefit more if she had taken it and that the benefits didn't outweigh the side effects. Since I am an oil painter, play guitar, and write for a living, these two women were all I needed for my ammunition for my own doctor. I prayed long and hard about that decision to stop treatments after only four appointments. I spoke directly to the doctor showing her my reason with printed-out statistics from Google, and she reluctantly agreed to let me stop. So, at this point, I only had three more chemo rounds to take and then on to radiation. This decision made me feel like either I was a brave warrior or perhaps the most stupid person on earth playing with my health in that manner. The oncologist was not happy at all with my decision. To me, it meant that I could get on with my *normal* life earlier than I had thought.

Speaking of this being a money game...I was so grateful for all of the precious nurses that would come by while I was hooked up to the chemo bags simply to ask if I needed something to eat or drink. If I had a headache from the chemo dripping into my port too quickly, they promptly offered me a Benadryl. It helped so much; until I got the bill from the doctor's office. Holy cow! Every pack of crackers or every coke was charged ten times the proper price to my account. Sorry if I sound like a skeptic, but that certainly infuriated me. I couldn't wait to leave. It felt like I was just a number.

As mentioned earlier, I lost my hair three weeks after my first chemo treatment. It had begun falling out in clumps. I had gotten my hair cut shorter a few weeks before so that it wouldn't be such a shock, but that didn't really help. I called my brother Scott to come and shave my head down to a buzz cut. He bought some clippers from Walmart and met me on my mom's back patio to help me do this deed. He laughed as he happily shaved my head as if he was having a ball. I was so grateful that T.G. was out of town as I didn't know how he would handle this new doo. He always loved my long hair. My girls thought it was so cool. We all plopped down onto the concrete and did push-ups like Demi Moore from the movie *GI Jane* when he was done. I have to admit, it was kinda cute, except for the blaring bald spot on the right side. I called Scott later that evening to thank him for doing this for me, and his wife said that he couldn't talk.

He was in the kitchen crying. She told me that it totally shook him up having to do that for me. I had no idea how much that experience affected him. I will forever be grateful for his help. I recall the texture of my hair quickly began to change, going from silky to feeling like mouse hair. It even started to change colors.

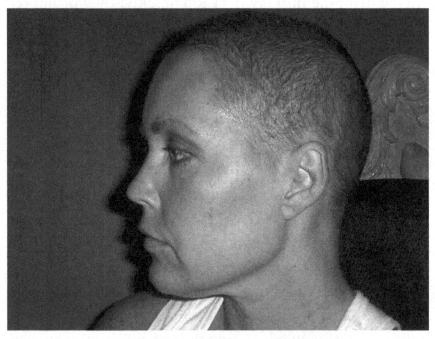

Kelly sporting her GI Jane look

I cried all of that night, harder than even the day I was diagnosed. Before my hair fell out, I could actually pretend that I wasn't this sick, but the second I lost my hair, it was the first outward sign that I was in a long hard battle. I had already picked out a few different wigs, but none looked or felt right. I was so insecure, and for some reason, I felt ashamed. How strange, I know. It wasn't my fault, but I felt tremendous shame.

I was grateful for friends that sent me cute bandanas and scarves so I could sleep without my head getting cold. I also didn't realize how painful it is when your hair comes out. It actually hurts to touch your head...like the nerve endings are on fire.

Speaking of Melissa Etheridge earlier, I was super impressed and blown away by her ability to perform at the Grammys without her wig. How did she find the courage to do such a brave thing? She became my breast cancer hero. It gave me the courage to think maybe I could do just that and perform without one of these stupid-looking wigs. Her courage raised more awareness for this dreaded disease in that show without her wig than if she had worn one.

I was scheduled to perform at the CMA Fest, the biggest gathering of Country music artists and fans, just months after my treatment. With Melissa Etheridge in my thoughts, I decided what better place to raise more awareness than here? At the beginning of the week, I sang on stage at the Wildhorse Saloon with Grand Ole Opry Star Jeannie Seely for a benefit for lymphedema, a horrible side effect of breast cancer. I couldn't think of a better place to begin. I felt naked but liberated as I sang to 1,200 loving and supportive people in this audience. I had just received word that my blood work was clear, and my radiation treatments were ending that week, so I asked everyone in attendance to help me celebrate. Lorrie Morgan was also there that night. She told me I looked like a Bad A--. I was thrilled. That evening gave me the courage to just take my wigs off completely.

When I finished my last chemo treatment, the doctor presented me with a diploma for completing my regimen. Since I hadn't actually completed all that she had planned for me, I felt like a phony accepting it. I really was a *Chemo Drop Out*. They all hugged me. Although they were very sweet to me, I hope I never see them again, no offense.

Jeannie Seely and Kelly performing at CMA Fest

For many months after my treatments, and surprisingly until this day, it drives me crazy when someone tries to compliment me by saying, "Well, you look good?" with a question mark at the end of their sentence. It is as if they expect me to be green and puny for the rest of my life.

Scan this code with your camera-equipped smartphone to view the bonus video. (Most IOS and Android devices can read QR codes by scanning with the built-in camera) If you do not have a QR app on your phone visit your app store and search for QR code reader.

10

CHEMO BRAIN

Chemo brain. What a funny term I began to hear a lot about those days, but I never actually believed it was real. It seemed like an excuse to make fun of someone or yourself. However, it *IS* a real thing. In my experience, it was very similar to the brain fog I had endured when I was pregnant. During this time, I remember that I would often forget where I had parked my car or what I went into the kitchen looking for.

Chemo Brain is the nickname of the fog and defragmenting that goes on in your thinking and speaking process when the chemotherapy drugs are in your system. I first noticed this becoming a problem for me three days into my first treatment when I asked my daughter, Payton (my oldest child), to ask Kennedy (my youngest daughter) to get into the dishwasher and dry her clothes. I was adamant and demanding that she did what I told her, and at the same time, was shocked when I audibly heard the strange words coming from my mouth. What I intended to say was, "Kennedy, please get into the shower and wash your hair."

Was I going crazy? Probably, but then again, I was under such stress and lots of pain pills. The kids just laughed at me, as this seemed to begin happening all of the time. I became embarrassed to even speak for fear of what might be coming from my mouth that didn't match what I was trying to say.

I would be at a restaurant and try to order a certain kind of food, like spaghetti, but it would come out like this: "May I have mayonnaise with a side of barbecue?" I was out of control; such a crazy feeling!

I had always been good at remembering before, but now I couldn't even remember people's names, numbers, and sometimes even forgetting entire conversations that took place. It was very similar to what I can imagine it must feel like to have dementia. This side effect gave me more compassion for others going through this stage of treatment. Please show others grace. We don't know what might be going on behind their smiles.

I made Nestle Tollhouse cookies one time at Mom's, as I was craving chocolate chip cookies every day at this point. As we began to eat them, I immediately realized that they tasted so bland and not as good as I had been craving. I had completely forgotten to put in the sugar! Everyone else got a laugh out of that but me. It made me sad. Not only did I feel like I looked awful, now my brain was sick too.

A few weeks later, I was craving a chocolate pie. I went to the store to buy the ingredients: Jell-O pudding and pie crust. It turned out to be a beautiful pie; I was so proud. My daughter started laughing as soon as she took her first bite. I joined in after taking a bite as I, too, realized something was wrong, yet again. How on earth could I have screwed up pudding from a box? All you have to do is stir in milk! An hour or so later, Payton rushed into my room, turned on the news, and said, "Mom, the newsman said that chocolate Jell-O Pudding is being recalled. They had accidentally put nuts in the box and called for all consumers to return it to the store for a complete refund." I was so relieved that it wasn't my chemo brain that messed the pie up this time. I was seriously beginning to worry about myself.

You know, even all of these years after chemo was in my body, still to this day, my thinking is not as clear or as quick as it was prior to taking the treatments. I've since had several conversations with other cancer patients that complain of the same experience.

Sometimes even today, I will be right in the middle of a conversation and get stuck on a simple word. I will stammer for a few minutes, clearly seeing the word within my head, and it just won't come to me. Thank goodness T.G. is patient with me and helps me figure out what I'm trying to say without making fun of me. When I get stuck, even all of these years later, he claims, *Chemo Brain* and we move on with a giggle.

I've also noticed a severe decline in my attention span. At one time, I was a book lover and enjoyed reading so much. I had a wonderful concentration ability and could remember everything I read. After chemo, I have hardly read a book and get very bored, finding it difficult to remember anything I read from the previous chapter.

I have also noticed a rapid change in my ability to remember where I put things. I may have always had a touch of undiagnosed ADHD, but it is out of control now. If I put anything into the freezer, and it is out of my sight, I will never, ever remember what I have in there to thaw out for dinner. I won't even think of going to my freezer. I just end up buying it again. I'm not sure if that is a symptom from chemo all these years later, but that is seriously how my brain has changed.

A little known fact about me though, while learning songs, I have discovered that if I type out a lyric, or anything for that fact, I have an extremely difficult time recalling what I typed out. However, If I physically write down what I want to remember, I have an almost photographic memory and will rarely forget what I wrote on paper with a pen. Isn't that strange? Does anyone else out there do this?

Scan this code with your camera-equipped smartphone to view the bonus video. (Most IOS and Android devices can read QR codes by scanning with the built-in camera.) If you do not have a QR app on your phone visit your app store and search for QR code reader.

11

RADIATION

Radiation is a whole 'nother animal. The gift that keeps on giving

A month after chemo had stopped, I had to start radiation. The doctors had warned me that since I had decided to keep my breast implants in, their treatment may or may not cause the implant to harden with time and may need to be removed later. I was willing to take that chance. They also made me sign waivers saying that radiation could cause cancer. Hmm, now that was a new one. Super confusing that they were trying to kill the cancer but may be causing more of it?

They put me through even more scans, measuring and marking the exact location where I was to receive the exact dose of radiation. Big black magic markers were used to indicate each spot, and then clear tape was placed all over my breasts so the marks wouldn't come off. I had markings all over my chest. I honestly looked like a monster, not to mention that I was already looking so beautiful with no hair. That same week, my lumpectomy site was swollen and had to be drained via a needle. I was so overwhelmed.

I have never even thought about getting a tattoo in my life, but the doctor insisted that I get a tiny little blue dot tattooed on my chest to mark the precise spot that they would direct their radiation each day. So, a tattoo I got.

Lying on a cold bed with my arm stretched over my head and holding onto a pole while my breast is exposed isn't a pleasant experience. A body cast was formed to fit my body perfectly to insure that I would be in the same spot every time. It was pretty uncomfortable. I thought it was ironic that when my hospital gown would fall off of my healthy breast, the technicians would gently cover that side up. I kept thinking, what is the difference? I'm already flashing you with one breast. They were very sweet.

I did a lot of praying during my radiation therapy (36 rounds in all). The daily treatments themselves didn't take very long. It took longer to remove my clothes and then get redressed again, but the drive to the hospital each day sure got old. I was always keenly aware of the other patients I would pass in the hallways on the way to their treatment and realized how much better off I was than some of them. I would say a secret prayer for each of them as they walked past me. I still do that to this day. Perhaps the best thing we can do for others suffering is to simply say a silent prayer on their behalf.

The radiation doctors had me add nine additional treatments to what had been scheduled initially because my tumor was close to the margin. The last batch was called Boost. The first five weeks consisted of radiation all over my breast, and in the last nine, they focused on the cancer site area. All in all, I did get burned but not as bad as I thought I would. I was afraid it would cause boiling blisters, as my friend had experienced in her treatment. I learned not to compare stories since every patient was different. I felt tremendous relief from using Aquaphor on my skin each night to ease the burning sensation. As a matter of fact, I still use it to this day. It is the most wonderful moisturizer on the planet.

I did have sharp, electric shooting pains periodically throughout my breast, but the doctor assured me that it was just nerve endings connecting. Lots of Aleve was taken during that time; it became my best friend.

I was sad that one of my favorite uncles from Oklahoma had died during my treatments, and I could not attend his service. My aunt, his wife, was a breast cancer survivor herself and totally understood. I was still mad that this stupid disease would keep me from such an important family event.

I have three aunts on both sides of my family that have gone through breast cancer. Actually, cancer runs in my family in a lot of forms. My oldest brother Scott had brain cancer when he was a baby. He wasn't given long to live but has since survived well into his 60's with five kids and a few grandchildren to boot. What an inspiration they all are to me. The way my sweet mother dealt with two of her children having cancer is beyond me. She is my rock.

During my very last treatment, I had tears of relief and joy roll down my cheek. I was given strict orders not to make a move, so I couldn't wipe them. Ahh, this was finally in my rearview mirror...or was it?.

Scan this code with your camera-equipped smartphone to view the bonus video. (Most IOS and Android devices can read QR codes by scanning with the built-in camera) If you do not have a QR app on your phone visit your app store and search for QR code reader.

12

HAIR TODAY GONE TOMORROW

I had some really big laughs during the transition from having hair to not having hair and all the in-between stages. Let me share with you the highlight reel.

One day, as I was at the YMCA, I went into the sauna. It was so warm and inviting. I was really beginning to enjoy and relax. A few minutes into it, I began to smell burning plastic. The lady next to me started holding her nose, and I knew it wasn't just me who smelled this awful scent. She pointed to my hair and said, "Honey, I think your wig is beginning to melt in here." I was horrified, but I had to laugh!

On another occasion, I had gone underwater during water aerobics, and my wig had come off in the pool. When I came up out of the water, there it sat, looking like an otter floating around me; so funny and embarrassing! I learned to have very thick skin.

I had an old Lexus 400 at the time I was going through treatment. It was a great car; however, it had a severe power steering fluid leak and would make awful moaning noises when it was low. Being on a tight budget, I didn't take it to a mechanic to have it fixed. There was also no way to keep the hood propped up while someone put the fluid in the pump, so it to be held up with a stick. One morning, I was in a rush to get my daughters to school, and I couldn't find my stick to hold up the hood. As the car was completely empty of fluid, I proceeded to hold the hood up with my head while gently pouring in the power steering fluid. The girls were sitting in the car impatiently waiting on me as I was running very late by this point. When I quickly got in, they both burst out laughing and asked me where my wig was. *OH MY GOSH!* We realized that it was stuck in the hood of the car. It must have come off when I slammed the hood shut!

Each time I would cook, this little wig would sizzle with the heat from the oven. I was so grateful to get rid of it after a while, but I am so thankful that it was given to me by the American Red Cross as a gift at the beginning of this whole fiasco.

One day, it was storming, and I didn't want the girls to have to wait out in the rain for the bus. I couldn't find my wig anywhere, so I decided to try out my new black doo-rag. It looked pretty stylish, I thought. Payton was so embarrassed for me to be seen wearing it in public but later told me that one of the kids at the bus stop said to her that her mom looked cool in her doo-rag, making me feel like a *cool* mom for a second. That feeling never lasted very long.

I recall lying in bed feeling my bald head. Normally it was so smooth and felt like a baby's butt, but on this day, I was so proud that I began to feel the first sprigs of new growth. I ran to the mirror and saw a faint shadow of hair that was starting to sprout. I looked like a chia pet. Everybody wanted to rub my hair, kind of like a woman's pregnant belly. After all, it was sort of like giving birth; I had been bald for months. I had become more comfortable with allowing T.G. to see me without a wig, and he had been so affectionate, rubbing my head each night while we watched TV. He told me later that although he would have never thought a bald woman would turn his head, he actually enjoyed rubbing mine as he loved how it felt. I secretly began to love it too.

As my hair began to grow out, I realized how much curlier it was than before. It was so straight before treatments, but now it felt like a poodle. I had no idea of how to begin styling it. I saw a fashionable-looking woman on the cover of a book around this time, and she had short curly bleached blonde hair. I thought, why not? It's now or never and, never would I have had the nerve to try this otherwise. I might as well play with this while I can. I bleached this new hair so white I looked like Billy Idol. It was a horrible mess, but I was proud to have been so bold as to try it.

I am not afraid to try anything anymore. After hearing that you have cancer, a little hair color change isn't near as scary as it once was. It's just hair, and as proved, it will come back! I realized that being a blonde wasn't in my best interest and immediately turned the color back to brunette, still wondering what was I supposed to do with all of these curls?

Lorrie Morgan, best known for her short and sexy hairstyle, was talking to me one day on our daily walks. She suggested that I get a flat iron and perhaps look in the store section that sold hair products for African American hair. I took her advice. While there, a beautiful woman of color was restocking the shelves and asked if I needed any help. She probably figured I was in the wrong area. I took off my red polo baseball hat and revealed my frizzy, curly mop, and told her I was desperate for some help in the hair department. She led me in the right direction. We talked for a few minutes, and I told her a little bit of my cancer story. She patted me on the back and said she would pray for me, sharing that her mother also had breast cancer. She then assured me that one day I would be able to laugh at this. I sure hoped she was right.

I went home and started to straighten my hair. Ooops, I mean, *fry* my hair. It looked like burnt cotton balls all over my head! At this point, all I could do was wet it, gel it, comb it back and let it dry with the wet look until it grew back. I was too aggressive, I guess with the blonde, then brunette, and then the flat iron. I was just so happy to have hair that I overworked it; typical for me.

A few months later, I strangely began to feel more and more confident with my new look. I began to get a lot of compliments from strangers saying how fearless I seemed in wearing my hair so short. I had always felt that Lorrie looked stunning with short hair and hoped maybe that was what people were beginning to see in mine. These people had no idea of what I'd been through, so fearless was not the word.

On the other hand, I recall eating at a restaurant called the Blue Goose and feeling pretty good about my short hair. I saw a group of young men walk in. One of them looked familiar to me, but I couldn't place him. He kept staring in my direction as if he might know me too.

As I was leaving the restaurant, I overheard him ask the waitress what was up with my hair. She leaned in, not knowing that I could hear them talking and telling him about my cancer. He coldly said, "I knew it had to be something. Why on earth would anybody pay for a haircut like that."

I was immediately cut to the bone and crushed with his cruelty. I hoped that the hair fairies would make him go prematurely bald. Mine would at least be able to grow out, but I had wished his wouldn't. In hindsight, it would have been great had I gone over to him and said that I had paid dearly for this haircut. People can be so cruel.

Now, when someone complains about having a bad hair day, I can remind them what a bad hair day really is. I am thankful for any hair that God will allow me to have without complaints.

As my hair grew, I asked Lorrie for more advice on hair products. I always thought her hair looked fantastic as it stood up like a rock star. She led me to get some spray gel called Pump It Up. She showed me how she would spray it on her fingers and dry it at the roots. I quickly began learning how to make my hair flip in the perfect way all over my head, kind of like Betty Boop. I was really beginning to enjoy this process more each day.

I was eager for my hair to grow as long as it was before. I quickly realized how hard that would be as it began to grow in different lengths. I woke up looking like I had an afro, but not in a great way. I started looking into hair extensions and weaves. *UGH.*

I was determined to try and get back to the person I looked like before, but after I grew it all back out, I realized that the once longer hair that I had gotten so used to didn't fit my spunky personality nearly as much as this new shorter style did.

Scan this code with your camera-equipped smartphone to view the bonus video. (Most IOS and Android devices can read QR codes by scanning with the built-in camera.) If you do not have a QR app on your phone visit your app store and search for QR code reader.

13

LIFE SENTENCE

A diagnosis of cancer in any form could be considered a *Death Sentence*, but I decided to switch the channel in my brain and consider it my *Life Sentence*. I took Tim McGraw's song "Live Like You Were Dying" quite literally.

Before my diagnosis, I'll have to admit I was rather selfish. If something didn't seem like it would benefit my family or me, I simply wasn't that interested.

I am guilty of having taken for granted that I would always be able to sing, travel, and be healthy. It is so humbling when you realize that nothing is a sure thing. We have all learned a bit of that lesson during the pandemic.

I was so busy as a single mother, just doing my own thing. The only real stress I had in my life at the time of my diagnosis was raising my girls. My life was pretty normal, I thought. I had resolved that my fun and exciting music career was just a hobby since I had spent so much time away from the spotlight to be a mom. I did, however, love it when I was able to perform from time to time.

Is it just me, or do we all have that period in our lives when we can put a pin on the exact time when something shifted in our lives? For instance, I bet most of you can remember where you were and how old you were when you heard Elvis had died. Or where you were when you heard about John F. Kennedy or Princess Diana's passing. I know I sure do.

Very similar to that, I will never forget the exact moment when I heard the dreaded news that I had cancer, along with the exact moment when I decided I was going to see it as a gift.

I am not going to lie. My switch of positivity didn't just happen overnight. It was subtle changes that all added up to a magnificent epiphany. For example, There was a window covered with mini blinds in the bedroom of my tiny condo, and at 6:00 am every morning, the sun would beam into my room, waking me up whether I wanted it to or not. I mean, it was so bright that I have even cursed at it before. The day after my diagnosis, the same sun, window, and blinds that I had sworn at previously, I now considered as a blessing and cherished. When you realize that you may never get to see the sun again, you then welcome it with open arms. It's funny how in just one day's time, I was able to change my perspective.

At the time, it seemed like I was at a doctor's office almost every day. As time went on, I realized that they needed to see me less often. Visits moved from every week to every other week; to monthly, then three months, to six, and then a year!

At first, I was just so hyper-focused on any change in my body. Every test I had to have and still have from that day forward, I know they are searching for some form of cancer. I now have to admit that I deal with PTSD from all of the MRIs I endured. The last one I had to have was just a few years ago, and it took four valiums to get me in the machine without having a complete breakdown. However, with each positive report that has come back over the course of several years, I have begun to feel a bit more steady on my feet. I told my friend, who is a few years behind me from her diagnosis, that this would happen to her also, and sure enough, it did. So, now I count every day that I don't spend in a doctor's office as a true blessing.

After getting a little more time behind me since my diagnosis, I became braver in trying new things like foods, traveling abroad more, or buying something that I just loved versus just what I needed. I also began using my fine china, and I burned my unused candles; before having cancer, I would have saved them both for *Special Occasions*. The difference in my attitude now is that I realize that just breathing is a *Special Occasion*.

I used to be more apt to say *NO* to things that I might feel would be out of my comfort zone. I now realize that living outside of your comfort zone is where true living really begins. One of my favorite sayings that I applied to my life around this time was, "Leap out into the abyss, and a net will appear and catch you!" Just knowing that my God would scoop me up in His Mighty hand if I dared to dream bigger for myself was so comforting, so I began to leap, and I leaped big!

My dear friend Jacy Dawn positively challenged me during this pivotal time. Although it had been a few years past my diagnosis, and I had begun to live a little more boldly, I still seemed to have a glitch in the personal confidence department. She is a brilliant marketing person and had offered to help me with putting together a new website. I secretly thought she was wasting her time,

Kelly and Jacy Dawn

but she said I needed it. Isn't it funny how others see you more clearly than you can see yourself?

Jacy came to Nashville from Massachusetts to pursue her dream to be in the music business. Although she is a wonderful singer/songwriter, her skills as a brilliant marketing person are off the chart. I'm so proud of the successful company she started called Platinum Circle Media and her new podcast *Country Music Success Stories with Candy O'Terry*. We have been dear friends for several years, encouraging each other to dream bigger. I love her to the moon and back, and I am so very blessed to have her in my life; I can't wait to see how far she will go in her own career.

I had been happy to live in T.G.'s shadow. I mean, after all, he was the breadwinner and had already accumulated 21 #1 hits. His income was enough to live comfortably on at the time, so it didn't make sense for me to be *wasting* money on a tired pipe dream. She kept pushing me. She said, "Kelly, I would help you even more, but I feel that you are holding back from really giving your career your all. You are 99% in but that 1% is making me not want to put any more time or effort into your career." Oh man, don't challenge an Okie. *GAME ON!*

I did some soul searching and wondered what it was that was indeed holding me back. It all stemmed back to confidence. I wasn't as young as I thought I should have been to compete fully; I wasn't as thin as the cute, hot girls that were younger than myself, and I hadn't made it any further in my career before that; so what makes me think I had a shot now? Was I going to make a fool of myself? All of these stupid insecurities kept running through my mind until one day, I realized that this was not how my Father in Heaven saw me. Doubt and insecurity come from Satan. I rebuked him that day and haven't looked back.

Of course, we all have days when we feel better about ourselves than others, that's just being human, but all in all, I am just doing me and am in my own lane. I don't even pay attention to any charts, who is playing what shows, or who's seemingly doing better than myself.

I began to celebrate others' successes. I might not have been that way before cancer, but I certainly am now. God revealed to me that there was enough room for everyone to succeed. If we feel like someone is doing better than us, it's easy to cut them down, However, if you can have a gentle change of heart and realize that particular blessing wasn't meant for you, it is life-altering. The more I genuinely began celebrating others, God made more room for me to receive blessings. The more I appreciated the small things in my life, God blessed me with bigger things. It became a fun game within myself to see how things would work out like that. I began looking around for someone at a restaurant, perhaps a woman eating by herself. I would secretly pick up her check, and then, the next day or so, I'd get a random gift card in the mail with double that amount as a surprise from a complete stranger. *YOU CAN'T OUT GIVE GOD!* He sees everything!

I also began a journal and started each day out with ten things I was grateful for. I challenge you to do the same. For example, note simple things like:

1. If you are reading this book, be thankful you have a computer, electricity, and eyes to read it with.
2. If you ate today, be grateful for every little morsel and for the ability to taste. There are some people that haven't even had a grain of food for days.
3. In light of the pandemic, that has made us all keenly aware of how much we took for granted. Heck, let's all be grateful for toilet paper here folks.

Seriously though, write down every little detail of what it is that you can be thankful for. You will soon see miracles coming your way.

I realized that once I took the focus off of myself and began showing love and compassion towards others, I became more peaceful. I challenge you to smile, even if you don't feel like it. Smile at someone in the check-out line. It's funny because a smile is infectious. If you smile at someone, they can't help but smile back. Even the angriest person will smile. If you are determined to smile, regardless of your situation, something happens in your DNA. It can force you into a better mood. (Believe me, there were times I didn't feel like smiling, but I did it anyway. I don't like taking medicine either, but I know it helps make us better...so *SMILE*)

Take it a step further and simply compliment a stranger. It costs you nothing, but may mean the world to someone who might be having a terrible day.

I've been accused of being Pollyanna-like. Ok, I'll admit it; I probably get that *glass half full* mentality from my sweet mom. She's always been able to give people the benefit of the doubt and sees the very best in everyone.

As life's lessons come around, I've learned to be a bit more cautious as to whom I trust, and the only adjustment is that instead of just being comfortable with my *glass half full* mentality, I choose to just refill my glass, to the top, overflowing. Our God wants us to live abundantly, and I certainly do.

When I say abundantly, it's not just material things I'm referencing; I look for reasons to appreciate everything more. I acknowledge the beautiful sky now, whereas I might have just overlooked it before.

You know, once you hear that you have the *Big C*, the scariest word in the world, every other fear you might have pales in comparison. I am not afraid of much of anything these days. Bring it on! I saw a great quote on JLo's page this week, and it really described my thinking to a tee. It said, "Once you become fearless, life becomes limitless." Oh, so true!

I am so appreciative to have met and worked with some of the greatest songwriters in the world. My dear friend Bruce Burch is no exception. He has written hits for Reba McEntire, "It's Your Call" and "Rumor Has It," along with T. Graham Brown's successful song "Wine Into Water."

Bruce had heard me mention the statement that I had turned my life from what some might think from a *Death* sentence into a *Life* sentence. He urged me on dozens of occasions to write this song with him. I was very reluctant to write it because I didn't want to draw the words into fruition. Sometimes as a writer, I've noticed that whatever I write about ends up coming true. Call me superstitious, and these words scared me to write, but I also felt compelled. Maybe someone hearing this song or reading these lyrics can gain some strength from them. Here are the lyrics to our song "Life Sentence"

Cold table, bright lights
Counting back from 10
Wake up from a foggy dream
Just to hear it's back again

Doctors paint the darkest news
But instead of death I'm gonna choose

A Life Sentence
But I am nowhere close to being finished
A Life Sentence
Now I'm living every minute
The things I took for granted
Mean so much more
Since I've just been handed
A Life Sentence

Bald head with a warrior scarf
Just to hide how bad it's been
Like a phoenix rising from the ashes
I will rise again
I will keep on fighting with a smile upon my face
With an attitude of gratitude
And God's amazing grace
He's given me a Life Sentence

I see the grass a little greener
And the sky's a lot more blue
And I love a little bolder
Ever since I got this news

Since I made the clear decision to live life more appreciatively, my entire world started to change. I started to attract more kind-hearted, compassionate people. Some that I thought were *friends* fell out of my life, but God replaced them with even more quality friends.

I began to create much more boldly and took chances in my career even more than before. To some people, it may look like I was just handed opportunities with my career or that I had a shoo-in with my connections, but that couldn't be farther from the truth. I have worked my butt off to get everything that has come my way. I had to struggle even harder to get ahead and learn to believe in myself, even more than I did before cancer.

I recall wanting to try out to be the opening act for a big country star (I won't reveal his name) after I had completed my treatments. I genuinely felt that I was up to traveling and would surely have enjoyed this opportunity. Before I was to audition, I was told that the star's wife felt that they couldn't take a chance on someone that had been so ill. She said, "What if she got sick and had to back out of the tour?" I felt so unfairly judged. I totally understood her point, but ironically that big star is no longer with us, and I'm still thriving.

I've always enjoyed traveling, so now, unlike before, when someone asks if I want to explore a new country, I am game to go. I cherish the memories I have created much more than I once did.

I want to encourage you not to wait until you've been given a bad report at the doctor to live like this. It is a gift for all of us if we are just willing to trust God, enjoy each day, and try to make the world a better place by being kind to others and even more forgiving to ourselves. Start today to live your *Life Sentence* so you won't have to be like me and learn it the hard way.

I often tell people that I'm frankly grateful for receiving a cancer diagnosis at such a young age. Being only 36 when I was diagnosed seemed like a horrible tragedy at the time; in hindsight, it has allowed me the rest of my days to see life in this beautiful and blessed way.

Scan this code with your camera-equipped smartphone to view the bonus video. (Most IOS and Android devices can read QR codes by scanning with the built-in camera.) If you do not have a QR app on your phone visit your app store and search for QR code reader.

14

LESSONS LEARNED

It's funny how something like cancer can bring along a certain fear in people around you, but it can also bring out a bit of appreciation. I realized some people that might have taken me for granted or had a bad thing to say about me before began to treat me much kinder. Perhaps they were trying to clear their conscience just in case I didn't make it. Since my announcement of this dreaded disease, I have been surprised by the reaction of others in my life. Some people I knew, and some I didn't, ran to my side to support me. Sadly, some abandoned me because of fears of their own.

There were times I just didn't feel up to answering my phone because I didn't want to talk about my health crisis over and over. This has given me such a clear perspective on how to allow others their much-needed space while they may be healing. I actually got tired of hearing about myself. However, I was always so grateful for those friends that continued to call and check on me. I learned

to delegate phone call returns to T.G. or mom when I
didn't have the strength to talk. I also discovered just
how important it was to me when someone didn't call
at all. Those hurt me a lot. Some of whom I considered
friends have never even called to see if I was dead or alive.
I have never been one to hold grudges, but it is hard to
forget. It is very important to acknowledge someone in
your life who may be going through a crisis, even if you
have no clue of what to say. My advice, just pick up the
phone and say, "I'm sorry. Is there anything you need?"
It goes a long way.

I had some wonderful surprises happen directly
because I was going through cancer. I didn't know if it
was just because people felt sorry for me or if they just
looked at me differently. Many people told me that I had
a serene and calm look to me and that I appeared more
beautiful now than ever. I knew they were just being nice,
but it was sweet to hear. I will say, in hindsight, after
looking at my pictures taken around that time, I did seem
to have a warrior radiance about me. Perhaps it was a look
of serenity on my face and God's peace surrounding me
that allowed me to glow from within.

I was shocked and flattered when during the time of
my treatments, hair barely growing back in, my art class
decided to paint portraits from each artist's point of view
of me dressed in a black halter. I believe there are about
12 similar paintings around town of me during this phase,
but I was excited when the teacher, Jennifer Simpkins
(Ralph Emery's daughter-in-law), gifted me with her
beautiful portrait. It hangs in my room even to this day,

and I wouldn't take a million dollars for that painting. It is a constant reminder of the warrior within me. All of these years later, I can admit now that there was a powerful glow to that young woman from a distance of time.

Oil painting by Jennifer Simpkins

I have never been comfortable with my looks or taking compliments well, but it seemed that I was receiving more and more since I had gotten sick. I figured people were just trying to make me feel better about myself. I didn't take any of their kind words seriously since I felt ugly and the scales showed I was much heavier than I wanted to be! I incorrectly thought that having cancer treatments would mean that I would lose weight! *NOT!*

I can say that the chemo treatments seemed very similar to being pregnant; in my opinion, I got the same cravings that I had when I was expecting. I craved spaghetti most days. I got heavier, moodier and I felt gross all of the time and extremely forgetful. Now when I look back on my pregnancy pictures, I admittedly see that undeniable glow. It was similar to this radiance that I recognized with chemo. You can not get that from any beauty product; it has to come from within. God provides that to us when we need it the most. I also felt a constant and beautiful sense of peace. Around this time, I was frantically looking for someone, anyone, near my age to ask for advice. I had aunts who were much older than me that have gone through breast cancer, but no one my own age. I tried to connect with a group of young women called Code Pink. Although they were precious and beautiful, brave young women, it made me feel even worse to surround myself with such depressing conversations. I loved all of their strength and hearing their stories, but it was too scary for me to continue hanging out with people who were much sicker than me. I wanted to surround myself with healthy and fun people. I had my head in the sand, I guess, but that was how I dealt with it. I also found myself not wanting anyone to bring me anything with pink ribbons or cancer-related things. Although I am grateful for all that people do to raise money for breast cancer awareness, I personally didn't want to focus on it. I wanted this to all be behind me. I was worried that if I hyper-focused on anything, it would bring it to me, and all I wanted was for cancer to disappear as quickly as it came.

I remember walking at the YMCA and witnessing a woman who walked daily with her father. She clearly was bald under her cool head scarfs. I heard through others that knew her that she had been pregnant when she was diagnosed. I was so shocked to hear that she had taken chemo during her pregnancy, but she couldn't do any imaging while she was carrying the baby. I loved watching her baby bump grow from afar. I took a few weeks off from walking as I was personally getting weaker with my treatments. When I returned to my walking schedule, I realized I hadn't seen her in a while. I began to ask around as to her whereabouts, only to hear that she had passed away; this was way too close for comfort for me. I cried for her and her family.

I also knew of a young girl in my town that had had a double mastectomy, and then the cancer came back in her collar bone before this young mother passed away. Although I felt terrible for her family, it also made me realize that I had been correct to have just chosen a lumpectomy over a mastectomy if hers had returned in her collar bone.

I was terrified even to have any conversation with anyone those days. I found that people, even with their best intentions, would say the scariest things. For example, "Hi, how are you doing? My mom just died of breast cancer, and I thought about you!" It would immediately put me into a panic attack. I couldn't be rude and act like I didn't care because, truthfully, I cared too much. I have had to learn how to process this info without taking it to heart.

A cruel aftermath of my illness is that I still experience panic attacks at the weirdest times that aren't even related to cancer, and I still cannot do an MRI without a complete meltdown. I now also freak out when I have to get IVs or have my blood drawn, as I am left with only one tiny, measly vein after chemo. However, that's still a great trade-off for all I went through.

I made a conscious decision during this time in my life. I promised God that if He could just heal me and get me past this, I would try and make a difference in people's lives by helping other cancer patients through their journey. I wanted to be a ray of hope for anyone that might be comforted by my story. I am a lightweight. If I can make it through something this hard, then you can too.

I hope that God is pleased with my efforts to hold up my end of the bargain and sees that I am trying to keep my promise. It is my passion to be a beacon of light for others, even if only to help and comfort them with my music or my story. I have been known to accompany friends to their own cancer treatments, although that puts me back into my panic stage all over again. I've learned to set safe boundaries for myself to be healthier mentally and or physically for others around me. One of my favorite things I've ever grasped in life was that the word *NO* is a complete sentence. It has helped protect me when I can't be all things to all people. God knows my true intentions.

One evening, I recall going to Gilda's Club in Nashville, an organization with locations throughout the U.S. founded in memory of the great comedian Gilda Radner from *Saturday Night Live*. She was one of my favorites of all time. Gilda had passed away years before with cervical cancer but was still making an impact with her life. The women hosting that evening allowed cancer patients to get free makeup and beauty advice. I did enjoy that lesson in learning how to apply makeup to my new blank canvas that once was my face. I loved that Gilda's legacy made women feel beautiful even in her death. What an inspiration she is. It inspired me to want to help women learn makeup tips too. That one evening gave me back some confidence, and I will forever be grateful.

Very much like Gilda Radner, I felt that I had to use comedy to keep it light-hearted for the others around me. Oddly, I felt the need to lighten the mood of others when I was the one needing lifting up. I thought that I needed to do whatever I had to do to make others around me more comfortable. I would say, "Oh, it's just a bump in the boob, no biggie," or anything silly to make others less afraid to speak to me and treat me as a regular healthy person. Oh, how I craved being normal again.

On the inside, I realized that this was indeed a serious situation. This was very scary to me, and I realized that it might not be the best solution for me not to honor the seriousness. I learned the hard way that it was not my job to carry everyone around me. For those that might have felt uneasy around me, well, they needed to work on their own fears themselves. It was not my responsibility anymore to cover for them.

One of the reasons that led me to cover my fear was caused by something that triggered my need to make light of it. I remember someone very close to me was so cruel. I confided to them how honestly afraid I was. Right in the middle of sharing how terrifying the possibility of leaving my girls behind was, this jerk told me to get over it, that we all die. Some people are so insensitive!

The other lesson I learned, which helped me deal with jerks like that, came from my friend, figure skater and Olympic gold medalist Scott Hamilton. He told me that when you come across someone who is apparently so miserable, just think to yourself, "I wouldn't wanna be them." I've had to use that a lot. There are many unhappy, opinionated, ugly-hearted people in the world. Thanks, Scott! That was a great lesson learned!

I'm such a natural caretaker in general, taking care of others before myself most of the time. But during this era, I realized that I have to take care of myself before I can truly be of any help to others. It's the same as when we are in an airplane, and they advise adults to put the oxygen on before attending to our children. At this time, I needed to do just that. I needed comfort, and I needed protection; for me to put myself first kind of upset a few people. It was a hard lesson that I certainly needed to learn. I realize that if we don't remember our lessons the first time we are being taught, the teacher will repeat the test. No thanks!! I got the message.

I understand that many women tend to put themselves last when it comes to nurturing their families/friends. During this time, I read a life-altering book called *Burnt Toast* by Terri Hatcher. The synopsis of her book was a simple but powerful lesson I'm proud to have passed down to my daughters and any other person that will listen.

As women, we tend to take the leftovers and give others the best of what we have to offer. For instance, if we were making breakfast and burnt the first piece of toast, we might scrape off the burnt side and not serve it to our children or husband; instead, we would choose to eat it ourselves. We then would make the most perfect piece of toast for our loved ones. This book challenged the reader never to do that again; to start expecting the best for ourselves as well. Never settle. Now, you don't have to be rude at a restaurant by being demanding, *NO!* You can simply ask kindly for what you ordered if it isn't what you really were hoping for. This simple example blew my mind! It changed the way I raised my girls, and I began to expect the best for myself. I started to look at my life through different eyes! I am a child of God, and He would also want the best for His children.

It has never been easy for me to receive gifts. It makes me so uncomfortable. Now, don't get me wrong, I love gifts, but the awkward feeling I get from not knowing how to repay the giver is what I'm talking about. The fact that anyone would take their time to think of me enough to send me something literally blows my mind!

During my cancer journey, I had to relax into the fact that some people love to give you things, or their time, to help ease the pain; it also helps the giver feel good. It was essential for me to continue being a stay-at-home mom to my girls. I lived very humbly and had already run through most of my savings account since being diagnosed. The misnomer was that people thought since I was dating a music star, that he was paying my bills. You have to understand, not only was T.G. dealing with his own financial crisis at the same time, I wouldn't ever have let him help me in any way. I had way too much pride.

Scared to death and with not much income coming in, I was surprised and comforted when I went to the mailbox one day to find a check for $1,000.00 from my sister. It was very unexpected and super hard for me to consider cashing, as I knew money was hard to come by for her as well. I called her to decline her generous offer politely, but she stopped me in my tracks with the lesson she began to teach me. She said, "If you allow others to give things to you, with an accepting heart, you are allowing the giver to be blessed." I had never thought of it that way. I immediately bent down on my knees and very humbly thanked God for my sister and for her much-needed help and advice.

Soon after that, I received a phone call from *Grand Ole Opry* star, Jeannie Seely, saying, 'Honey, I know life is hard for you now, and you don't need to worry about your bills on top of your health. The Opry Trust Fund wants to help you pay your living expenses until you get on your feet!" I no sooner got off the phone from talking with her when a call came in from another organization called Musicares. They said that country star Marty Stuart had called them on my behalf saying that whatever the Opry fund wasn't able to pay, that they would! Wow! What a double blessing. What did I ever do to deserve such generous gifts? A woman from the Opry Trust Fund even fought with insurance companies on my behalf to help get my bills down, and we all know what a nightmare that can be. I was way too weak to fight those battles, and I so appreciated her help.

I even had a total stranger come and clean my condo so I wouldn't have to. How nice was that? The simple fact that someone cared enough for me to get my groceries, or to take my children to school, send a card, or prepare a meal, all small acts within themselves, were so enormous to me and so appreciated.

Since I was trying to cut financial corners anywhere I could, I needed to quit art class. I was sad because that was a wonderful and relaxing outlet for me. I so appreciated my art teacher offering not to charge me for classes for a few months until I got back on my feet. She knew how much I needed that creative release.

See, no matter what we do for others, it can seriously make a difference in how someone heals. It doesn't always have to be monetary help. Having gone through cancer has definitely opened my eyes as to how I can be of more service to others needing help. I can honestly say I was genuinely unaware of how to do that before. It has made me a more compassionate human being for sure.

Scan this code with your camera-equipped smartphone to view the bonus video. (Most IOS and Android devices can read QR codes by scanning with the built-in camera.) If you do not have a QR app on your phone visit your app store and search for QR code reader.

15

DREAM BIG:

THE POWER OF A WISH BOARD

One of the gifts I received on my 40th birthday literally changed the course of my entire life. I was sitting on the floor of my condo opening my presents after the party, and I got to the last gift. It was a DVD called *The Secret*. I thought, "That's weird." Thinking it was such an odd gift, I put it aside for a few days. Curiosity was killing me; I mean, what's the big secret? I put it into my DVD player, and it began with such mysterious music and information that I had never heard of before. The gist of it is all about the law of attraction. Whatever we concentrate on and think about will come to us. This idea was nothing new as I had already known that prayer does the same thing, but this was explained in a way I had never heard before.

One of the guests on the DVD suggested getting very clear about what we want to attract into our lives and prompted viewers to make a Wish Board. He suggested putting a picture of your dream car, your dream home, or vacation. Whatever it is that you desire, you must feel what it feels like to have it already. Ok, I didn't have anything to lose at this point, so I took the challenge.

I had to sell my beautiful baby grand piano after my divorce and had always wanted another. So, I cut out a picture of a black baby grand piano and pinned it to my board. I had wanted a white Jaguar car, but I couldn't find a picture of a white one, so I just put up a pic of the first one I could find; which happened to be silver. Since I had gotten an appetite for traveling abroad, I decided I'd love to see more of the world. I put different iconic locations I'd like to visit like Buckingham Palace, The Eiffel Tower, The Sydney Australia Symphony Hall, and Venice, Italy. I also put up a beautiful white house with specific dramatic details to the roofline.

Most importantly, after seven years of dating, I really wasn't getting any younger and wanted to be married. So, I put a pic of a bride and groom. At this time, I wasn't sure if T.G. would be the groom, so I just showed the back of the couple in the picture.

I hung the wish board up and prayed over it, releasing all of these things to God.

Wouldn't you know, within three months, T.G. and I began talking more about marriage. We looked around for homes just in case that was ever to happen, and to my surprise, he proposed right there in the bathroom of my favorite home we looked at; not a super romantic proposal, but I should have been more specific about what I wanted huh? We were married on August 20, 2007. I later looked back on my wish board to take off the pics of the bride and groom and realized that I was also in a home that looked almost exactly like the house I had put on my board. Ironically T.G. did buy me my dream car, but it wasn't white...oh no, it was silver! You have to be very, very specific as to what you put on your wish board. With all of this in mind, I thought, when will my wish piano arrive?

I am so blessed to report that since putting all of those amazing locations on my wish board, we have been fortunate to visit every one of those places. First, for our tenth anniversary, T.G. and I decided to take a trip to London, where for a tiny sliver of time, they were allowing tours through the inside of Buckingham Palace!

Buckingham Palace

We took a quick train ride over to Paris, where we dined on the top of the Eiffel Tower! We took that dream trip to Australia and not only saw the Symphony Hall but also went to the Australian Zoo, where my other dream was to hold a Koala

Bear. Then ultimately, we rode a gondola in Venice, Italy, with dear friends Kim and Greg Fannin. It was the most fantastic trip ever!

Eiffel Tower

Australian Zoo

Italy

The significant part of all of this is in hindsight, if I hadn't dreamed of going, put it on my wish board and thought about how important it is for us to make as many memories as we can while we are still on this earth, none of these trips would have happened.

We are so grateful that we took the time to see all of these magnificent places before the world shut down travel abroad. I am not telling you this story to brag about our lives. I know it is expensive and lavish, but if that is truly your passion to see more of the world, you can and will find the means to go. It is life-altering! Just try my suggestion, cut out pictures of places you'd like to visit and picture yourself there. It will blow your mind when they come to fruition! Think about it like this, if you never put your order in at a restaurant, you'll never get your food. If you put it on your wish board for the places you'd love to see, your chances of getting there faster are way higher. Whatever you focus on will come to you much quicker.

On another note, what negative thoughts you tend to focus on will come to you as well, such as "I don't know how I'd do that" or "I don't have the extra money." I have learned that it is not our business to figure out the how-tos. It is up to us to trust God to deliver.

Be very careful at what you put your intentions on. Think of a race car driver. If he was to focus on the wall instead of the track, what do you think he will see first? Speak only positivity over yourself. Don't talk about an illness like it is Your cancer or Your back problems, *NO!* Say I *had* cancer or *A* back problem, Don't label yourself that way. I put the word *HEALED* on my wish board and the word *Content*, and I choose to focus on those words all of the time.

I don't look at my wish board as anything against prayer. *Oh No!* Quite the contrary. I look at it as a form of keeping my focus on what I have petitioned God for and then being overwhelmed by His desire to fulfill whatever we ask for. Just like a parent with a child, I want to give my children the desires of their hearts, but until they tell me what they want, I'd never know what to give to them. God wants us to live abundantly and will give us what we ask if we are obedient to him. Remember the bible verse that says, "Ask, and you shall receive?"

I kept shopping for pianos, but the price of a baby grand was more than I was willing to pay, as I didn't know how often I'd actually play it. For some reason, the word *Knabe* kept running through my mind. At the time, I had no idea what that word meant. I googled it and couldn't believe that it was a piano company that just happened to be 20 minutes from our home. I immediately called them to see if we could tour their plant. They agreed. A wonderful man named Jay Cross was there to greet us. I told him that I was a writer and had a lot of artist friends that came to our home for sing-alongs. I asked if they ever did sponsor deals with artists. He excitedly agreed to send me not one piano but two! They were installed within our home that very day! Later, we would have all of the artists who came to our home sign our piano, and then we auctioned it off for charity. The piano I have now, though, I sang at a convention for Knabe pianos in return for this incredible gift. Since I began having artists sign my piano, I am happy to say that we have the Oak Ridge Boys, Brenda Lee, Dave Ramsey, Jeannie Seely, John Rich, Mac Davis, John Conley, and more. My two favorites, I must say, are the last ones before the pandemic when Sir Barry Gibb and Dame Olivia Newton-John signed my piano with "To Kelly, Love and Light, Olivia Newton-John," and Barry wrote, "Me Too, Barry Gibb."

The night Barry and Olivia signed my infamous piano was so special. Barry was in Nashville recording his duets album called *Greenfields*. It is a wonderful collection of Bee Gees songs re-recorded by mega stars of today with Barry. He had invited Olivia in to sing with him. We all decided to get together for dinner, but it is very difficult to find a private location where they wouldn't be bothered. I recommended our home as I was happy to have everyone over, but I soon panicked. I'm horrible in the kitchen! What do you cook for such special guests? Since they are both world travelers, I wanted the food to be perfect. I just called in for a variety of different types of food to take the pressure off. They all began to arrive at our home; Barry and Linda Gibb, his manager Dick Ashby, their daughter Ali and then Olivia and her husband, John Easterling. My mom and her boyfriend Paul were there as well. We all sat at our kitchen table reminiscing and enjoying each other's company for hours.

The highlight of the evening was gathering around my piano for a sing-a-long. Harmonizing to old songs is always fun, and we do it almost every time we get together.

Since Barry had recently become knighted by Prince Charles, his new title is Sir Barry, and his adorable wife is now Lady Linda. I was also aware that Olivia had desired to be a Dame, the equivalent of a knighthood in England, but that honor had not been bestowed upon her at the time of this dinner. She had been given the highest award in Australia, but it isn't called a Dame. As a small party gift, I had hand towels made with everyone's new titles monogrammed on them; Sir Barry, Lady Linda, Dame Olivia, and her husband John is known as Amazon John. They all seemed tickled with their gifts and admitted to keeping them on display later in their bathrooms. Olivia later called me so excited to tell me that she indeed was getting ready to be made a Dame soon after that night, and my towel must have been a prediction of what was to come. How sweet of her to let me know. I am so excited and proud for their well deserved honors.

L-R: Lady Linda Gibb, T.G., Sir Barry Gibb, Kelly, Amazon John and Dame Olivia Newton-John

As they are all such kind and loving friends, I don't get too overwhelmed anymore about how big of stars they are, but when I think back, the fact that I was truly entertaining royalty in our home is mind-blowing. Coming up, I'll tell you how we met Barry and Olivia. Just hang on...

Another unusual thing that I had wanted so badly and had put on my wish board was a swimming pool. I *LOVE* water and I missed having one. The home we were living in at the time didn't have a big enough area for a pool to be built, so T.G., who is not a pool guy, was somewhat relieved. I was desperate to have one, but I also realized that it was an extra expense we probably didn't need. However, I kept dreaming and looking at the beautiful pool on my wish board daily.

One day, I said, "T.G., if I got a free pool, you couldn't say no, right?" He just laughed, knowing I was surely up to no good. I had called a company named Viking Pools and asked them if they would be interested in a sponsorship plan with someone in the country music field. When I told the lady I was speaking with T.G.s name, she was so excited. She had grown up on his music and had hoped to have someone in Nashville promote their pool company. Well, we needed an actual backyard for that... oops, I hadn't thought that far out yet!

We were made aware that our favorite home, owned by our dentist (in the neighborhood we already lived in), was coming up on the market. We quickly made plans to buy it. Within a month, actually on T.G.'s birthday, Viking pools hovered our *FREE* pool over our house into what is now my happy place. Not only did they provide the pool, but they also installed an iron fence, the surrounding pavers, a gas grill, a fire pit, and aquatic exercise equipment! I soon realized that when you begin dreaming bigger for yourself and really learn to focus on what you want, it becomes easier to manifest your dreams more quickly.

Anyone who knows me well knows that my pool is my sanctuary and where I am relaxed enough to write my songs. For those that follow my social media pages, I'm sure you've seen pictures of dragonflies landing on me when I'm in my pool. The backyard is also filled with gorgeous redbirds that swoop overhead. It is where I feel the most serene.

Now, my challenge to you is to go and put a wish board together! Dreams really do come true, but remember to DREAM BIG!

Have you ever experienced the phenomenon of numbers showing up in your life at the most unusual times? I sure do! Ever since I was a young girl, my dad would make a point to call us kids when he would see 11:11 on the clock to tell us that he loved us. I thought that was just a sweet thing within our family. Come to find out, that number is pretty significant to others as well. I see it ALL of the time now, especially when I'm trying to make important decisions. It will show up on a receipt at a restaurant, or flash on my alarm clock even when it isn't 11:11! I have heard it is supposed to be angels letting you know you're on the right track but I also like to think of it as my dad still watching over and guiding me. It brings me great comfort whenever I see it.

Kelly and Conway Twitty

Loretta Lynn and Kelly

Kelly and George Jones

Garth Brooks and Kelly

Kelly and Mac Davis

Wynonna, Kelly and Naomi Judd

Kelly and
BJ Thomas

Lionel Richie
and Kelly

*June Carter Cash
and Kelly*

*Vince Gill
and Kelly*

George Strait and Kelly

Crystal Gayle and Kelly

Buddy Hyatt and Kelly

T.G., Ronnie Milsap and Kelly

*Larry The Cable Guy
and Kelly*

Trisha Yearwood, Kelly and Don Henley

Scan this code with your camera-equipped smartphone to view the bonus video. (Most IOS and Android devices can read QR codes by scanning with the built-in camera) If you do not have a QR app on your phone visit your app store and search for QR code reader.

16

IN SICKNESS AND IN HEALTH

August 20, 2007, was one of the greatest days of my life. After seven long years of dating and wondering if this wedding would ever happen, T.G. and I were heading to the altar!

I had been so ready for this day to come. It didn't feel like I thought it would have in my mind. I thought I'd be super nervous and anxious about every detail. Instead, I'd never been more calm and relaxed.

We had never lived together before our marriage, so moving the three of us girls into the same house with this bachelor was going to be quite an adjustment. T.G. spent the night at a local hotel the night before the wedding, and my girls and I stayed at the new home where he had proposed a few months before.

The following day I recall us girls going to IHOP for breakfast and then to Walmart to pick up a few last-minute items for the ceremony.

I had bought my beautiful wedding gown at a consignment store. My daughters picked it out for me. It was white satin with a taupe sash down the back; nothing too fancy. I wanted our wedding to be casual and elegant, and it sure was.

The Happy Couple

We were so happy to have our wedding in the backyard of dear friends Cecelia and Flavil VanDyke's gorgeous lake home in Gallatin, at the Fairview Plantation.

They lived in a southern mansion with a pool and amazing gardens surrounding the entire property. The exact spot where we said our vows was a fancy gazebo overlooking the lake at sunset. My daughters and T.G.'s son Jason stood up with us. Our friend played T.G.s song "Finally" on his guitar as the kids walked towards the gazebo. As my brother Scott walked me down the aisle on that hot but beautiful day, a bagpipe player played "The

Highland Cathedral." It was magical, like a movie. The ceremony was short and sweet. We filled a glass vase up with different colored sand representing each one of us in the family, which still remains in our bedroom. We let white balloons fly into the air after our vows. It was beautiful.

We looked around that day into the smiling faces of our supportive family and friends. Some of the artists that were in attendance were the Oak Ridge Boys and Lorrie Morgan. It was small and quaint, but the love felt that night was enormous. I was thrilled to "Finally" call this beautiful man my husband.

Lorrie Morgan, Kelly, T.G. and the Oakridge Boys

The evening continued with music, finger foods, and desserts. For some reason, I was adamant about having a dang chocolate fountain. Cecelia tried to warn me against it. Oh, how I wish I had listened. The second I got a strawberry dipped under that fountain, a blob of chocolate splashed across the front of my dress. I was so happy that night, I didn't really care. In fact, it is so typical of me to make messes wherever I go; I never even got the stain out of the dress to this day. It is a funny reminder of that otherwise perfect event.

The limo brought us to our new home, and T.G. tried his best to get me and that dress over the threshold of the door. We laughed as he eventually put me down inside the doorway. We opened our wedding gifts for hours and giggled at what we had just done. I was in heaven.

We celebrated our honeymoon at the Cloisters hotel in St. Simon Island, Georgia, an amazing gift from sweet friends Alan and Trish Welch.

A sweet side note - on our 4th anniversary, T.G. hired the same bagpipe player to serenade me on our front porch! Super romantic!

Prior to our wedding day, T.G. and I had already been through what our vows would tell us to do as a married couple:

- Sickness and In Health, CHECK!
- Richer or Poorer, CHECK!

We came to the conclusion that if we could make it through both Cancer and Bankruptcy, along with him being a new step-dad to my two little girls, we could conquer anything!

I learned a lot about him very quickly that I didn't know before. This man *HATES* glitter! Boy, did he marry the wrong girl - I sweat glitter! I was wrapping his Christmas gifts while he was on the road. I knew he'd be coming home shortly and wanted to get them all under the tree. He came home a few hours early to surprise me and saw that I was knee-deep in Christmas bow glitter. His reaction was hilarious! He began to vacuum around me and didn't even acknowledge how pretty his gifts were. It would have hurt my feelings if I hadn't thought he was so funny. From that day forward, I always choose the most glittery of paper or bows to see how he will react. He must have given up by now because he just laughs it off. I must be his worst nightmare!

I believe the secret to our successful marriage lies in our not taking ourselves too seriously. We are always laughing or finding humor in the most serious of things.

I am quite aware of T.G.'s success in the music business, so I know that there is never a feeling of competition between us. I love how supportive he is of my career as well. He says that when he sees me getting to do exciting things within my work, it's almost like living his life all over again vicariously through me. I lean on him for guidance, as our careers are very similar, but I appreciate that he also relies on my advice. We are the very best of friends.

My favorite thing about him is that he is the first to apologize if he is wrong. That is an excellent quality. I'm still trying to learn that one. I am also keenly aware that he had a life before me, and I'm not putting my head in the sand about his past; heck, I had a past too. I just want to share with you the man I know now, today, and hopefully, till death do us part.

I feel that I have overstayed my welcome when it comes to health issues. Cancer is rough, don't get me wrong, but the after-effects from the treatment seem to never go away.

Five years after radiation, I decided it was time to remove my breast implants completely. They had been so affected by the radiation that they had hardened like rocks within me. T.G. was so kind and supportive of that decision. Within a few days of the surgery, something was seriously wrong as I had a gaping open wound under my arm that was leaking a strange colored fluid. I went to the surgeon to check it out and was immediately admitted into the ICU with a staph infection. T.G. had to seriously work his magic to allow them to let me go home. He totally stepped up to the plate as my 100% caregiver and was responsible for changing out my IV bags twice a day for eight weeks. A nurse would come by the house once a week to check on him, and he got an A+ from them. I was so grateful to be home under his care.

I thought that having my implants removed would be a complete turn-off for him. I was thankful he kept telling me that he wasn't a *boob guy*, but knowing how kindhearted he is, it was hard to believe him; this made me super paranoid and depressed. I was so deflated and now disfigured. I had to heal for another year before I could do any repair.

I first tried fat grafting, taking fat from my tummy to fill in the disfigured breast. That was a total failure. I then tried implants again, being that they now looked like a lumpy mess. Unfortunately, the doctor who came highly recommended decided that he knew what was best for me and just did what he wanted. I specifically told him before surgery that no matter what you do, *PLEASE* do not cut me from my areola down to underneath my breast. I just never wanted that scar to show. Guess what? He cut me there anyway! That made me *soooo* mad! The side that was healthy to begin with, and never supposed to be scarred up, now looked worse than the side that had cancer! *UGH!*

I left them that way for a long while, and I tried every scar cream known to man, but for some reason, that scar began to keloid. That's when a scar looks more purple, thickened, and raised. Oh great!

I chose to go to a female plastic surgeon the next time. Her name is Dr. Lois Wagstrom, and she is a miracle worker. I think it truly made a difference when I chose a female doctor because she understood how important this was to me.

Unfortunately, those implants hardened and had to be removed within a year. Here we go again! I tried this implant thing once more in December of 2020. So far, as of the writing of this book, I am very happy with the results. They were able to laser that ugly scar to where it is barely noticeable. Since there were so many surgeries on my breasts throughout the years (I honestly have lost track of how many breast surgeries I've had just to get back to some semblance of normal), my areolas began to lose shape and were not the same size or color. I know this is too much info, but for anybody that has gone through this before or may be going through it in the future, I am your guinea pig! Perhaps the reason I had to go through all of this was to help someone reading my words. I am happy to report that with tattooing, my breasts now look like they did when I was 35! No kidding!

I was told that health insurance is quick to pay for breast surgeries for cancer patients because they know that there will definitely be more surgeries in the patient's future. The radiation is the gift that keeps on giving, in the fact that it basically cooks you for years from the inside out. Who knows, I may have to have more reconstruction done in the years ahead, but for me and my 35-year-old looking boobs, we are gonna just be happy for now. By the way, T.G. now claims to be a boob guy! *Wink, wink!*

You may be asking yourself, "At this age in your life, why would you keep having surgery on your breasts?" or "What difference does it make to have them look perfect?

You should just be happy to be alive." For those of you
that have not had this experience, I am sure these seem
like logical questions. Let me explain it this way: If every
time you looked in the mirror, you saw a reflection of
scars reminding you of the most horrific and scary time
in your life, and if there was something you could do to
feel better about yourself, wouldn't you want to do what
you could to try and repair the damage from this terrible
disease? I bring this to your attention to let you know
that breast cancer survivors do not undergo these surgeries as a form of vanity. It is a choice to try and restore
our lives and something that you have to walk through
personally to understand fully. To fellow survivors, if you
have an opportunity to have these types of surgeries, do
not hesitate to have them. I encourage you to embrace
the choice and if you come across any judgment, dismiss
it and whoever passes it.

Another gift I received from chemo and radiation that
I hadn't expected was weaker discs in my back. I knew
going into those treatments that there may be side effects,
but I had no idea they would be years after my treatments
were over. A disclaimer, my family has a history of back
problems, so I'm sure that had something to do with it
as well.

One day I was unpacking my suitcase after a trip to
Florida. I simply bent down to get my pajamas out of
my bag, and *BAM!* I was lying on the floor screaming; I
couldn't move! T.G. rushed me to the hospital, where they
treated me for a ruptured disc. The pain just wouldn't go
away for weeks. We finally had an MRI done that showed

the problem. I decided to call my friend, country star Larry Gatlin to ask his advice since he had just had laser back surgery in Houston, Texas, by Dr. Aloe. He suggested that I go there instead of trying a traditional back surgery approach. I took his advice. I had to be wheeled through the airport in a wheelchair; it was so embarrassing. I met T.G. in Houston as he was flying in from a concert to meet me.

Not only did I have one disc blown, but five! I had two different back surgeries within two days. The recovery was brutal. T.G. again was so precious to me as I healed. I had to wear a neck brace and back brace for weeks; super sexy. The nerve damage that resided in my foot for years afterward was excruciating.

I don't tell my personal medical issues to have anyone feel sorry for me—quite the contrary. On the outside, I looked like a healthy, strong girl, but I was very broken physically, and because of that, I was also feeling broken mentally. People may have thought I had it all together, but I was just holding on by a thread some days. I want you to be aware that everyone, no matter who they are, is going through something that you may never know about. We need to have more compassion and kindness for everyone we see. Let's begin to lift others up. They may be having a horrible day, and your kind words can literally change their world! You'd be surprised to know that everyone is hiding a scar of some sort, whether it be physical or mental. I have scars all over me, but you'd never even know about them unless I were to tell you.

Please be kinder to those you run across, and even more so, be kinder to yourselves.

I'm so grateful that God knew what He was doing when He brought T.G. into my life. I seriously don't think I'd even be alive today if not for him. In sickness and in health, till death do us part.

Within our many years together, T.G. himself has also had some very serious health issues arise. I have learned so much from him about properly taking care of your spouse when they need you the most. It is my great honor to be by his side to comfort him when he has been sick, as he has done for me.

If T.G. goes before I do, I can tell you I would certainly be one lost girl, and only then will I need y'all to feel very sorry for me. I don't think I'd ever remarry. He has broken the mold, and because he has spoiled me so much, he has ruined me for anyone else that may come along.

Scan this code with your camera-equipped smartphone to view the bonus video. (Most IOS and Android devices can read QR codes by scanning with the built-in camera) If you do not have a QR app on your phone visit your app store and search for QR code reader.

17

STAYIN' ALIVE

I had been contracted to do a few shows before being diagnosed and I was determined to follow through with my commitments. One of these shows was in Northern California. T.G. and I had been booked to perform together at a festival, and we so looked forward to the getaway. As we got onto the plane, we realized our seats were several rows apart. This was so disappointing. He asked a few people if they'd mind switching seats, but nobody was willing to offer. I sat in the back row, and he was three rows in front of me.

I was getting so irritated with him, seemingly so happy to visit with the lady next to him. What on earth could they be talking so much about? I couldn't see their faces, but I heard them laugh a lot. As I was sitting with my face looking out the window of the plane, I found myself feeling very lonely. This show was only the third time I had been on stage since going through cancer, and I felt very insecure about performing with my cropped haircut. I was exhausted and not even sure I wanted to sing anymore. I truly had just wanted to take a nap on the flight leaning into T.G., but fate obviously had a different plan.

As we landed in California, all of the passengers were hurriedly grabbing their bags to leave the plane. T.G. excitedly waited for me to get closer to him and this mystery woman he'd been so friendly with. Her name was Marianne, and I have to admit she was precious. They had been talking about all the people in Nashville they may have in common. She proceeded to tell him that her daughter had recently been diagnosed with cancer. I was embarrassed that T.G. was so willing to share my cancer story with a complete stranger. All very random points in the conversation, but they all would begin to make sense much later.

We exchanged numbers, and many months later, I went to lunch in Nashville with this kind and fascinating woman. I had invited her to a concert I would be perform-ing at the following month at a renowned Nashville club called 3rd and Lindsley.

She and her husband came to my show, and while there, for some reason, she kind of blurted out to me that she knew Barry Gibb's secretary. So random, I thought, but was it? Weirdly, I had just told T.G. a week before that I felt very strongly that I would become friends with Barry Gibb. Now, what on earth made me say that or even have that thought was beyond me, but I just knew it was going to happen. I had heard on the news that Barry had recently bought the house formerly owned by the late

Johnny Cash, which was just down the road from where I grew up in Hendersonville.

Several months pass and then on April 7, 2006, nine violent tornadoes touched down in middle Tennessee. This horrific cluster of storms killed many in our surrounding towns and was life-shattering for everyone in our close-knit community.

We were all in shock, and I felt like I needed to do something to help. However, having just completed my treatments from cancer, T.G. discouraged me from taking on too much. He didn't think I was strong enough to handle the pressure of putting together a benefit concert I had started working on.

I was thinking back to an unusual conversation I had a few months before that kept nudging me to go forward with this enormous undertaking. I was on stage with my short new hairstyle in Wooster, Ohio, just going through the motions to fulfill my contract; I couldn't wait for this show to be over. I was insecure and not strong enough to be on the road yet. However, God had a reason for me to be there, that I know for sure.

While signing autographs after the show, a middle-aged man came up and spoke to me. He said, "Miss Lang, I am the chaplain of the Wooster Police Dept. I have a message that I've been told to relay to you from God." Now, that's enough to get your attention! This is the second time that God has sent someone to give me His message. Wonder why He didn't just talk to me Himself? I'm going to ask Him that one day. I proceeded to put my sharpie down to listen intently. He had very kind eyes, and he was very adamant that I listened to his instructions, ensuring I received this important message.

He said that I was born to be a celebrity and that I would soon be on a stage where the audience had no end. I wouldn't be able to see the number of people I would reach. (At the time he told me this, we didn't have Facebook, Twitter, Instagram, etc.... so this seemed very farfetched.) He proceeded to tell me that my breast cancer was all going to be ok, but it had to be part of my story so I could help others. He also told me that Satan would try to hurt me and give me doubt, but God would help me fight him. I said, "Yes Sir."

I didn't even ask questions. I knew in my spirit that he was indeed correct. I felt a strong sense of peace, and I thanked him for this revelation. I'm not saying that I felt deserving or worthy, but I did feel honored and willing. To be sure that I wasn't dreaming this all up and not wanting to forget any detail, I asked that he please repeat the message for T.G.; I'm so grateful that he did. Now when I get scared or doubtful, T.G. always reminds me of that memorable conversation. We know that God's hands are on us, leading our every move. I feel that my breast cancer has been a gift in a strange way. If God thinks enough of me to bring me through it and trusts me to fulfill my promise to help others, I don't want to let Him down.

I can now look back on this conversation, and in summary, I feel like my music career has offered me a bigger platform for people to hear my real message of hope. I've never been moved by money or fame, but helping others has always been a passion of mine.

I proceeded to put together the benefit concert we called *A Night Of Healing* within days of these horrible tornadoes. I felt an urgency to help. Since we live in a town filled with such amazing musical talent, I began to reach out to our friends who lived in the area.

William Lee Golden of the Oak Ridge Boys home had been destroyed, so you can imagine how surprised I was that they were one of the first to agree to perform.

Everyone was willing to sing, including Lorrie Morgan, The Oaks, Ricky Skaggs, Gary Allen, T.G. Sheppard, and more. We were excited that the great Ralph Emery agreed to host. A full-circle moment for me, as the concert took place on the football field of my high school in Hendersonville. There were so many sweet people that volunteered their time; I couldn't possibly remember all of their names. The United Way stepped up to the plate to help with the organization of the details. This benefit was all put together within three weeks. That is unheard of! We ended up raising close to $100,000.00

During the planning of this show, I was awakened in the middle of the night with an epiphany. My inner voice, which I think is God, told me to contact Barry Gibb! *WHAT?* I don't know him! I don't know anybody that knows him...oh but wait! Maybe I do! I texted Marianne and asked, "didn't you mention to me that you knew Barry Gibb's secretary?" She said "Yes." I told her that I wanted to invite him to our local benefit. I mean, who knows if he was even going to be open to that, but I thought I'd ask.

She gave me her friend Liz's email. I was very nervous writing this message, but felt strongly compelled to send it. I questioned back and forth as to whether I should or not, but hey, the worst that could happen is that he might decline. One of the lessons I have learned in my journey is that the answer is always no until you ask, and so I did. My letter went something like this:

Dear Mr. Gibb,

I know this is a long shot, but I wanted to reach out to see if you may be interested in helping out with our benefit concert to relieve people who were affected by a recent tornado. I know you've bought the Johnny Cash home, and who knows, you may be visiting your home during this time. If you are available and interested, I'm not asking you to sing, but it sure would mean a lot if you'd be open to just waving at the audience, your new community.

Some of the artists that will be on that night include, (I listed all of the artists)

Thank you in advance,
Kelly Lang

Imagine my surprise; a few days later, as I was driving through the McDonald's drive-through getting my favorite ice cream cone, my phone rang with a number from Miami that I didn't recognize. I reluctantly answered and heard an English accent. It was Barry's manager Dick Ashby saying that they had received my email, and strangely enough, Barry was indeed going to be seeing his home for the first time that exact weekend. He proceeded to tell me that not only would Barry be willing to come and say hi to his new community, but he wanted to sing with me! *WHAT?!?!?*

Sir Barry Gibb and Kelly performing at
A Night Of Healing

We quickly made plans for my guitar player and me to meet him at the Cash home for rehearsal. I thought I was going to die with excitement. We arrived at the house and were quickly led to June Carter's old room, and right upon her canopy bed sat the *BEE GEE* himself; Barry Gibb, wearing a straw hat, holding a guitar, and he greeted us so kindly. He was so sweet and friendly. As he strummed his guitar, he began to hum "Mee, Mee, Mee" in his famous falsetto voice. Maybe this was what heaven was going to be like, I thought. We ran through his infamous song "Islands In The Stream" a few times. I asked him what had made him agree to sing on this show, as he had not performed for awhile. He said it was *Serendipity* and that he felt we would be friends for life. If T.G. hadn't been there to witness that, I would feel silly saying it out loud. However, I did remember telling T.G. that we would be friends one day. My, has that come to fruition!

I was delighted to meet his gorgeous wife that day at his home. Linda Gibb is a stunning, exotic-looking woman with a beautifully wicked sense of humor. We hit it off immediately and on a profound level as we both had dealt with cancer in our pasts. We remain extremely close all of these years later.

T.G., Kelly, Lady Linda and Sir Barry Gibb

After that wonderful evening, we have made many trips to visit Barry and Linda in Miami (I'll tell you a funny story about that later). We've gone to Disney World with their family and even traveled to Australia with them to see where the Bee Gees grew up and began their career. We joined Olivia Newton-John while over there as Barry was singing with her for her Olivia Newton-John Hospital and Wellness Center. Traveling with both of them in Australia is literally like traveling with royalty.

One of my favorite memories with Barry has to be when he invited me to perform with him at the induction of Kenny Rogers into the Country Music Hall Of Fame in Nashville. Since we had performed at a few events already, (at a diabetes benefit in Miami and in West Palm Beach for another occasion), he became comfortable singing with me; what an incredible compliment!

Kenny Rogers and Kelly at his Hall of Fame induction

Being that I was around country music since I was a child, I was excited to see everyone, but I felt extremely comfortable around them. I didn't realize how much he looked forward to meeting the likes of Bobby Bare, Allison

Kraus, Emmy Lou Harris, and all of the others there on that program. The truth of it all is that every artist there was in awe of meeting *HIM*! As a matter of fact, when we got off stage, even Garth Brooks said, "Kelly!!! You just sang with Barry Gibb!" I was happy to introduce him to Barry. His Nashville community instantly embraced and adored him.

I got very emotional when we walked out on stage, and I saw Kenny Rogers himself sing along to our version of "Islands In The Stream," a massive hit that Kenny and Dolly Parton had made iconic in the day. The very next night, Barry and I performed on the Grand Ole Opry together. Career Highlights for sure.

Sir Barry Gibb and Kelly (Grand Ole Opry)

About a year into our friendship in 2007, a tragic event happened. The famous Cash house that the Gibbs had begun remodeling burned to the ground. As everyone in town knew that we were friends with he and his family, I was urged to call him with the horrible news. I reluctantly did, and I could hear the heartbreak in his voice. He and Linda had beautiful plans for that estate to be a second home for their family. Barry wanted to make it a place where he and his Country Music friends could write and continue the legacy that Johnny Cash had begun. I remember the fire trucks arriving to help put out the ravaging fire. The unique, wooden A-frame home was having some final touches done to the floors. Unfortunately, the product used to varnish them caught on fire when a torch (being used to work on some plumbing) sparked a flash fire and engulfed the home instantly. I looked around to see the sad faces on the neighbors as this historic site went up in flames. We were all so grateful no one was hurt.

As an entertainer, you know you've made a name for yourself when they paint a caricature of you and then put it on the walls in a famous restaurant chain called The Palm. In Nashville a few years ago, Barry was honored with his painting, and T.G. and I were so happy to come to the unveiling. Imagine my surprise in 2012 when I received a call inviting me to come down for the reveal of my portrait. It just so happened that

Barry and Linda were in Nashville, so I was excited that they could be here to celebrate with me. I was tickled that the Palm decided to put me next to T.G.'s place of honor on the wall. So, if you're headed to the bar, turn to the right, and check it out! You can't miss us.

While finishing up lunch at the Palm that day, I told Barry how much I loved his accent. He said "Thank you, and I love yours too." I quickly told him that I do not even have an accent. Without skipping a beat he said something

I apparently say a lot. In his best southern accent he said "Bless Your Heart!" We all cracked up!

Several years later, we were visiting Barry and Linda at their home in Miami. It was the first time we had stayed with them there. I was told we were staying in the same room that Diana Ross and Michael Jackson had previously slept in. That was cool. I had a hard time calming down to sleep that night. A weird fact about me: when I get overly excited or nervous, electrical things go awry around me. I have a hard time with watches keeping proper time; even my cell phone sometimes sends me emails from the year 1969, and light bulbs blow out all of the time.

I Googled the weird phenomenon regarding this electrical problem some of us have. It is supposedly an electrical malfunction in some people. These people are called *Sliders*. I've been told that I need to be more grounded. I prefer flying, thank you very much. I digress...back to my story.

On this particular sleepless night, I had already taken off my makeup and was in my pajamas, just drifting off to sleep. All of a sudden, I was awakened with fire alarms blaring. We were shocked to see Barry himself checking in on us in the room. We looked out to see fire trucks arriving. *OH NO*, I thought! Not another fire I was going to witness. If you know anything about the Gibbs, everything makes the news! I sure didn't want to be evacuated in my pink pajamas and no makeup. I quickly ran to get dressed and put on my face when the alarm went off. We were all so relieved that it was a fluke incident. In 43 years of living there, the Gibbs said they had not once heard that alarm in their home. T.G. was quick to teasingly blame me for being the culprit.

I am so very grateful to call Barry and Linda and their wonderful kids our extended family. They are more precious than rare gems to us, and we cherish every moment ever spent with them. Some of my most beautiful times have been just hanging with Barry and Linda. Doing nothing with them is just everything. I love them with all of my heart.

Reflecting on a conversation I had with my oncologist, I had just celebrated my 40th birthday. It was a "Stayin' Alive" theme party where I was dressed like John Travolta and asked others to dress in 70's themed costumes. We played disco music and danced all night. I thought it was super clever to have named the theme of my birthday "Stayin' Alive" since I'd recently gotten to know Barry. I also felt it appropriate in light of my cancer battle that I was determined to get past.

During my oncologist's appointment, I told her that I was sad that she hadn't been able to make it to my party. I mentioned to her how grateful I was to even be celebrating my 40th party, as I hadn't been sure I'd even be alive to do so. She coldly told me that she had been pretty confident that she could get me to my 40th but wasn't so confident in how much longer I'd survive thereafter.

That comment and a few other negative ones throughout my treatments led me to fire her. Yep, I didn't even know you could do that, but I had the confidence to take my own life into my hands. I chose never again to allow anyone, including a powerful doctor, to speak any negativity over my life. Best decision I ever made.

What Sir Barry Gibb says about Kelly Lang

"Knowing Kelly for the past several years, she has become a beloved friend and a part of our family. She bears the glow of creativity, and whenever she walks into the room, it is obvious to everyone. From writing beautiful songs to painting pictures from her heart, she is a true artist in so many ways. There is only one Kelly."

Scan this code with your camera-equipped smartphone to view the bonus video. (Most IOS and Android devices can read QR codes by scanning with the built-in camera) If you do not have a QR app on your phone visit your app store and search for QR code reader.

18

I HONESTLY LOVE YOU

Six-year-old Kelly with Dame Olivia Newton-John

Sitting in the audience in Oklahoma City was a six-year-old superfan of Olivia Newton-John. As her career was unfolding as a country star with such hits as "Let Me Be There" and "If You Love Me Let Me Know," I sang to the top of my little lungs along with her. I felt an instant connection to the beautiful Australian singer. I was so excited to meet her after her concert.

I recall wearing my red, white and blue outfit, the best I had in my closet, to greet my idol. She looked adorable in her blue jean overalls. I had never met anyone from Australia before and was mesmerized by her darling accent.

Just a few years later (we had already moved from Oklahoma to Tennessee as a family), the iconic musical movie *Grease* was released. I was so happy to see this classic motion picture in the theaters the very day it came out. What an awesome movie! I, like most of you, have seen that movie now probably hundreds of times. I always loved Olivia's portrayal of Sandy, the innocent schoolgirl, but I loved her sexy version of Sandy even more.

Fast forward a few years. Olivia's career had taken an even sexier turn when her song "Let's Get Physical" came on the scene. I think it's funny now that it was considered so racy at the time that a few places even banned it.

I was in the audience in Murfreesboro, Tennessee when she brought her *Let's Get Physical* concert to our area. I loved her *SO* very much; I showed up with my new Olivia-inspired short haircut and my coolest headband in her honor. Wow! What a great memory.

I had every album she ever made and sang along to them in my bedroom pretending to be her. Every boy in the world probably had a huge crush on her outer beauty. I just wanted to be more like her because I saw something beautiful within her spirit. Her voice was so angelic, and her vibe was so amazing.

After my friendship began to unfold with Sir Barry Gibb, he had invited us to be his guests at a charity event, *The Love Hope Ball,* for diabetes research in Miami, Fl. in June of 2007.

Imagine my enormous surprise as I was sitting at the table waiting for the event to begin. A woman behind me tapped me on the shoulder, wondering if she could sit at our table as she waited for the show to start. Unbelievable! It was *HER*!!! She was scheduled to perform with Barry at this event. He hadn't thought to tell me that Olivia would be there, rather less sitting at our table. I almost died. How on earth did I ever get this lucky? Thank you, *GOD*!

She was even sweeter than I had ever thought she would be. To then meet her as an adult was such a full-circle moment. I could leave this story right here, and that would be enough for me, but no...

The very next day, during lunch at Barry and Linda's beautiful home in Miami. Linda just happened to mention who all was coming over to eat. When she said Olivia and John, I thought, "No way...did I just hear her say Olivia will be joining us? You've got to be kidding me!!" I tried to squash my excitement, and I feel like I did a pretty good job. They arrived, and everyone hugged and welcomed them in the door. She came over and hugged me and was so warm. We all ended up in the kitchen helping Linda prepare a few things. Linda had mentioned that I, too, was a breast cancer survivor.

Olivia was so interested in my cancer journey. I remember her asking me if I had done chemo and radiation. I told her that I was supposed to have eight chemo treatments, but I decided to drop out early. She was so quick-witted. She broke into "Chemo Dropout" to the tune of "Beauty School Dropout" from her famous movie, *Grease*. We all had a good laugh. She was so engaging and fun. We seemed to hit it off very quickly. As the evening came to a close, we exchanged numbers. I was thrilled, but I honestly didn't think I'd ever hear from her again. To my excitement, she called me a few weeks later, and that began a lifelong friendship.

A year or so later, we were all back at the Gibb's home again, but I was a bit more at ease around her this time. My favorite memory from that night was when we all gathered in Barry's media room and sang old country songs together. I recall "Help Me Make It Through The Night" and Olivia singing beautiful harmony with me, T.G., and Barry. What a blast!

Dame Olivia Newton-John and Kelly

She and her wonderful husband, Amazon John Easterling, joined T.G. and me in Florida for the gorgeous wedding of Barry and Linda's son Michael. Although the ceremony was spectacular as all of the Gibb men wore kilts, I had the most fun the next day. The Hard Rock Seminole Hotel, where we were staying, had a great shopping area, and Olivia had called asking me to join her. We had a blast going from one store to the other. We went into one of our favorite stores, where they had some beautiful sequin jackets. I was so ecstatic that she bought me one as a gift. I loved it so much. How generous she is. We totally bonded as girlfriends even more, as only shopping with friends can do.

T.G. and I were so happy to join Olivia, John and their other close friends at their home in Jupiter, Florida (the same neighborhood that Celine Dion resided in), to celebrate John's birthday. Their home was magnificent, so warm and relaxing. How sweet to see our picture together on her entryway table.

She and John kindly agreed to allow a film crew and me into their home to film a pilot about their love of pets. I was so impressed with their passion for each other and their love of their beloved Irish Setters. I painted portraits of them as a gift. She still has them hanging in their California home with their collars on them all these years later after they passed.

In 2015, Olivia invited Barry to sing in Australia for her Olivia Newton-John Cancer and Wellness Center. T.G. and I were also asked to join them all over there. Wow, what a fantastic experience being in their home country with them both, a true chance of a lifetime. I so enjoyed riding around with Olivia seeing where she attended school and some other noteworthy places she grew up around. She and Barry sang "How Can You Mend A Broken Heart" that evening as a duet. I loved their version so much; I put it into my memory as a moment to never forget.

We never really talked much about music or the business, but Olivia did ask me what type of music I sang. I reluctantly sent her an album of mine called *Shades Of K*, a collection of vintage songs recorded to lush tracks. She was so complimentary of my low ranged vocals. Funny, I always wished I could sing higher like her!

I'm so glad that I followed my gut to send her my music, as one day after her performance with Barry in Australia, she called me out of the clear blue, and during our talk, she said, "Are you planning on recording any more music like your *Shades Of K* again?" I said, "Well, yes, I have actually been in the studio already doing an album of some classic songs that I didn't get to record on the last project." Teasingly, I said, "Wanna sing a duet with me?" She immediately replied, "Sure, what do you want us to sing?" I quickly added, "I want to record the same version you and Barry just sang in Australia of "How Can You Mend A Broken Heart." My goodness, where'd that come from? I didn't even skip a beat!

She loved the idea and agreed to meet me in Studio At The Palms recording studio in Las Vegas. I had already laid the track with my vocal on it in Nashville. Olivia had already been performing in Las Vegas but was still living in California at that time. I later found out that she flew in a day early just to record with me. The track ended up on my album entitled *Throwback*.

I have always had a passion for classic songs, so years ago, I decided to share my love of them each week with my Facebook fans and called it Throwback Thursday. Every Thursday, I would tell the viewers interesting facts about the song I was going to sing, like who wrote it, what year it came out, and something about the artist that recorded it. I would then get my guitar and sing these awesome songs to the best of my ability. I am not a great guitar player, but I had hoped that my love of this music would resonate in my voice.

I truthfully had *NO* idea how many people were listening to my videos until I flew to Australia to meet Barry and Olivia. To my surprise, I attended several places, and different people called me the "Throwback Thursday Girl!" Until then, I naively thought that the thousands of viewers watching those videos were just numbers, not real people. I then decided to make a CD including some of my favorite songs from the series of videos and entitled the album *Throwback*.

I was also honored that Lee Greenwood and Paul Shaffer from *Late Night With David Letterman* joined me on duets within the same album. Olivia was so kind to help me promote the project.

Kelly and Lee Greenwood

To my surprise, she has included our version of "How Can You Mend A Broken Heart" on her CD, *Just The Two Of Us: The Duets Collection*. Never in a million years did I ever think I'd become friends with her, rather less get to sing with her. Now to be included within her remarkable album alongside the likes of John Travolta, Barry Gibb, Paul Anka, Dolly Parton and Mariah Carey, just to name a few!

One very fond memory of Olivia was when T.G. and I were getting ready to perform in Laughlin, Nevada. She was just visiting Vegas before she signed on for her residency and invited us to come over to the Flamingo and hang out with her and John. We had a great lunch there in the suite. Her dog Raven had to go out for a walk, so T.G. and I joined them. We were sharing with her that we were not used to singing duets together, and somehow we always messed up, making it more nerve-wracking. As we were headed back into the lobby of the Flamingo, right there on the steps outside, she began to give us stage tips.

"Ok, T.G., you stand there, and Kelly, you stand there. Now when the verse starts, Kelly, you cross in front of him. T.G, when Kelly is there, dance with her a bit." It was so funny! She gave us such important, simple tips that we still use to this day! After all, she is the most iconic duet partner in the world! What an unbelievable memory of her teaching us. If the people walking around her that day realized who she was, they would have flipped out! Of course, they would have never thought they'd see this megastar just out walking her dog or giving stage direction to us.

We went to see her perform in Vegas several times and were so appreciative that she had put a picture of us within her montage of photos alongside other celebrities before her show would begin. She is such an outstanding performer and singer. I'm amazed that she still sings in the exact same keys as she did when she started her career.

I adore our friendship and look up to Olivia as a big sister. I have talked with her about some of the most personal things. She has such kind, funny wisdom that I have been comforted by on many occasions. I love that she is so genuinely supportive of other female artists' careers.

We have so much in common, like motherhood, being female artists, mutual friends, our love for animals and, being cancer survivors, or as she likes to call it, *cancer thrivers*. Of all the famous people I have ever met, she is who most people want to know about. I don't talk much about our relationship because it is so precious to me, but I wanted to include her within this book as she has been such an inspirational radiant light for me to follow. I hope to have learned how to do that from her for someone that may be reading this book.

Although she has had some serious health issues with breast cancer recurrence, I've yet to see Olivia without a smile on her face. She is seriously the most positive and uplifting person I've ever known. I love her courage to take her health into her own hands and look for natural ways of treating cancer. Her husband, Amazon John, is well known for his knowledge of medicinal plants and has been successful in treating her cancer for years. They are true pioneers for how this disease can be treated successfully, and I'm so very grateful for how well John has taken care of her. They are both marvelous friends, and I'm forever thankful for them both.

Olivia is one of the most iconic artists of all time, but I love her most because she is so kind and humble. Her quick wit is phenomenal. If I could model my life after anyone I've ever met, it would certainly be her.

It is super flattering to get a message from her regarding my music. She told me that she plays my CD *Old Soul* for her dinner guests when she entertains. Now that is something I am proud to put in my baby book.

A fun fact about the album *Old Soul:* It was released on September 18, 2020. A few days before, I appeared on *The Huckabee Show* to promote the album. To my honor and surprise, the City of Nashville and the City of Oklahoma City declared September 18th officially as *Kelly Lang Day*. Subsequently, Governor Huckabee also presented me with a beautiful award to celebrate my induction into The Oklahoma Music Hall of Fame.

Kelly and Governor Huckabee

Another treasured memory with her was when T.G. and I were performing at the Florida State Fair. Olivia called to see what we were doing for Valentine's Day. She and her husband

John happened to be a few hours away from where we were. They drove over and spent the entire day with us. She and I walked arm in arm throughout the fairgrounds. I loved going into the animal petting area where I watched her pet a baby goat. I was soaking in my time with her, as we, unfortunately, live far apart and don't get to see each other as often as I'd like. Everyone was excited to meet her, yet she just wanted to talk privately with me to share some recent health knowledge she had learned and felt that I needed to know.

One very exciting time was when she was doing *Grease Singalongs* in Florida. T.G. and I flew down to join her. This is where the fans get to sing along with the movie and act out some of the scenes with props . To their surprise, the stars of the movie come out on stage afterward for a Q&A. It was so much fun!.

The night before the show, Olivia invited us to a wonderful dinner. Other guests at the table were Sir Cliff Richard, some of the T-Birds from *Grease*, and then walked in the great John Travolta himself! I am such a big fan of his from *Grease* and specifically, my all-time favorite movie *Urban Cowboy*. He was such a sweetheart.

Kelly and John Travolta

Remember, I don't let opportunities pass me by anymore, so I asked if he would take a picture pretending to dance with me. He did even one better and said, "Why should we pretend?" He swung me around and then dipped me! I've never been the same ever since; I love my life!

And I Honestly Love Olivia Newton-John.

What Olivia Newton-John says about Kelly Lang's Album *Old Soul*

"From the moment I put on Kelly's CD, I smiled!
You know when you hear a song on the radio and
you have to turn it up so you can hear it properly?
Thats what I felt about this whole CD!
From the first song to the last I kept smiling!
A wonderful selection of popular songs perfectly
suited to Kelly's beautiful and unique voice. She
can sing anything from country to jazz to rock!
I love how she switched Mrs. to Mr. Jones in the
song "Me and Mr. Jones"
Kelly's voice is warm and inviting, sharing her
heart in every song- and I love that she sang
"Quando,Quando,Quando" the only duet with
her talented husband T.G. Sheppard!

Scan this code with your camera-equipped smartphone to view the bonus video. (Most IOS and Android devices can read QR codes by scanning with the built-in camera) If you do not have a QR app on your phone visit your app store and search for QR code reader.

19

MAKEUP AND WARDROBE

I am always so flattered when people reach out to me for beauty or makeup tips. I am certainly no expert in that field. However, I do totally enjoy the ritual of all things cosmetic. If I hadn't ended up being in the music business, I certainly would have gotten my cosmetology license. I always loved that Tammy Wynette kept her beauty license up to date just in case her music career hadn't panned out.

I worked part-time at the makeup counter in Dillards when I was also singing on *The Ralph Emery Show* and took great pride in being the top seller there. I love helping women be their very best.

When I went through chemo, I had lost all of my hair, eyebrows, and lashes. I don't care how much I tried to hide the fact that I was going through cancer treatments; there was no getting around the inevitable loss of hair. Eyebrows frame the face, and lashes extend the eyes to make them more appealing and protect the actual eyeball. I felt naked. It was a very vulnerable feeling. I may be considered shallow, but don't judge me until you've walked in these shoes. For my personality, who loves all things glamorous and pretty, I felt very raw and ugly.

I slowly learned this new me and tried my hardest to use tricks to fill in the brows and grow my lashes back. Trust me; my brows, lashes and skin were never the same. I felt like I had aged 20 years with all of the chemicals they pumped into me. My hair was a completely different texture. I had to really get to know new products all over for this new me. The old Kelly was still alive and kicking inside, but the mirror reflected someone quite different.

A few months before my diagnosis, I began to use Cindy Crawford's skincare line, Meaningful Beauty, and had gotten so many kind compliments on my complexion. I had reached out to the company to tell them how much I loved their products. They were so kind to send me a few month's worth of their skincare and mentioned that they might consider using my testimony to promote their line. As I was going through chemo at this time, I called to tell them that I was probably not the best candidate to endorse them. However, they kept sending me Cindy's cosmetics and then came out to my home to film me and my daughters for their upcoming commercial. They loved that I was still radiantly glowing even during treatments because of their skincare line. When the actual commercial came out, I was embarrassed that all they showed was a clip of me saying, "My friends thought I had gotten botox, but all I used was Meaningful Beauty." I can't tell you how many people reached out to me all across the country about my tiny part within that commercial. I still stand behind this exceptional product.

Since growing a bit mature (notice I didn't say older?) I realized that my skin had gotten much drier. I love using coconut oil all over my body and face after my showers. It is like eating 12 avocados; good fat. I also love a good natural exfoliant, so I use plain old cornmeal in the shower to scrub off any dead skin cells before I apply the coconut oil. It is a cheap, easy fix for all that ails you.

My makeup drawer is insane; I always love trying new trends. I subscribe to Ipsy, a makeup kit that allows me to sample new things I might never have known of. For just $10 a month, a decorative bag arrives filled with five selected products. I am like a little kid at Christmas, so excited as I try each new product.

At this time, I am really enjoying *It Cosmetics* and *Milk* makeup. I would not have known about either one of those if not for the Ipsy bag. Another favorite brand I love is called *Cat Cosmetics* by actress Catherine Hickland. All of her products are of such high quality. I encourage you to branch out from your everyday routines and try new things to keep your look current; maybe go to the makeup counter for a tutorial or advice.

I don't claim to know everything. Makeup or skincare is a lifelong journey since styles change and new products are recreated or invented every year. Also, our skin changes with age, requiring new ideas to keep us at our best. I am trying to be more natural with my daily looks, allowing my skin to breathe when I am not working, but you will never see me without something on my face to at least enhance my green eyes. I also always have a shimmery lip gloss in my purse. I don't care what the trend is; I am a shimmer girl. Some say that makeup is like putting a mask on to hide our natural flaws or that wearing it is a form of insecurity. I have been either accused of wearing too much or admired for knowing how to use it. Some judge me for not wanting to be seen without it, and some just want my opinion on how to apply it. Either way, it is a hot topic, both good and bad. I simply can put a stop to the judgment and say I thoroughly enjoy makeup and how it can enhance a person's beauty. I can be feeling blue about myself, but then apply a nice lip gloss and automatically feel better. I find nothing wrong with that. It is a quick and easy pick-me-up that I highly recommend.

One of the highlights of my entire life was regarding makeup tips. Let me expound by sharing a funny story. Years ago, I received my very first royalty check from BMI for writing a song. I was so excited with my .63 cent check. I was about to get it framed when I realized that it wasn't even written out to me, but instead to actress Katherine Kelly Lang from *The Bold and The Beautiful*. How humiliating it was to have to send this back to BMI. A while later, I accidentally ran into her co-star at a party and told him about the funny mixup. I asked him to relay to her who I was and looked forward to meeting her one day. He had her call me. She was a sweetheart. Since our names are the *same*, we have since gotten mixed up on many more occasions.

The most memorable mixup was when I was in Las Vegas. I was celebrating my friend Jacy's birthday, and we had a night there before I was to record with Olivia Newton-John the next day. We decided to attend *The Donny and Marie Show* at the Flamingo hotel. I enjoyed their fantastic performance. What awesome entertainers they are. I was shocked when, at the end of the show, Donny said, "We are so excited anytime celebrities come to see our show and tonight is no exception. Would you please welcome, from *The Bold and the Beautiful*, actress

Katherine Kelly Lang!" What are the chances of that? I excitedly looked around to find her to no avail. Marie said, "Donny, you goofball, it's not Katherine Kelly Lang! It is country singer Kelly Lang!" I had no idea she even knew who I was, so it was a double shocker for me! We were able to have a private meet and greet backstage, where Donny profusely apologized, and Marie and I cemented a long-term sisterhood/friendship.

Marie Osmond and Kelly

Marie and I realized how much we had in common. We both have been performing since young girls, our dads were both in entertainment management, we both had been divorced and single mothers, we had several friends in common, and we both loved makeup! Marie, being the only girl in her family, was very easy to become girlfriends with.

After her show one night, she and I were in her dressing room, and she said, "Kelly, the next time I see you, I want to do a makeup tutorial on you for my Facebook page." I honestly didn't know what made her want to do that. Was I so hideous that she felt sorry for me? Did she secretly want to fix what she didn't like? So funny how our insecurities play out in our heads, huh? I reluctantly but excitedly agreed.

The next time I was in Vegas, sure enough, one hour before her showtime, she and her makeup artist Kym sat me down at her makeup mirror and began to transform my face. She introduced me to her millions of fans as her girlfriend; and proceeded to make me into *Elizabeth Taylor* with her makeup tricks. I was shocked when Donny Osmond himself crashed our Facebook tutorial. He didn't say this, but I think he was in shock that Marie had never done makeup on anyone else but herself before, so why me?

L-R: Marie Osmond, Kym (Marie's makeup artist)
Donny Osmond, T.G. and Kelly

Her makeup drawers were filled to the brim with the most expensive items and multiples of each. She was so generous to teach me things I've never known before. It was like opening up the Holy Grail of makeup knowledge. She taught me the importance of contour, proper ways of lip lining to change the shape of the entire mouth without lip fillers and, how to apply false lashes. Most importantly, she explained the need to have fuller eyebrows, as they give us a more youthful look. All of this happened *LIVE* in front of the world. It was a true out-of-body experience I will never forget.

I teased her and asked if the reason she had wanted to do a makeover on me was that she felt sorry for my stagnant makeup. Being such a supporter of all women, she said, "No, she just thought I was beautiful and wanted to help enhance what I already had going on." Although I hadn't noticed because they were on my own face, my brows must have still had a remnant of being too thin from chemo because that was what she focused on. It was life-altering. Marie has no idea how much her kind compassion and knowledge seriously changed my way of doing my everyday makeup routine. I think of her each time I sit in front of my makeup mirror and smile. As a matter of fact, I want to share my latest wild hair. Ever since having chemo, my brows have never been the same; so sparse and hard to fill in with makeup. My lashes were less full, and my eyes always looked weak. Since I don't want to go out without something on my eyes, I recently decided to take the plunge and get eyeliner and eyebrow tattoos. This has rocked my world! I can now wake up feeling like I am almost all ready for the day. I highly recommend this to anyone wanting to spend less time in the mornings getting ready, like me.

To make a full circle, thanks to social media, I have now become closer friends with Katherine Kelly Lang. We both laughed at how having the same name has altered my life with Marie.

On occasion, I enjoy doing makeup tutorials on Youtube. It wouldn't be right for me to keep the valuable information that I've been taught over the years and not share it with anyone that might be interested. Marie taught me to be generous with information as to help others.

Before cancer, I always felt a bit too indulgent to make self-care a priority. Truthfully, I was too broke and stressed financially to take good care of myself. I didn't have the extra resources for facials or massages. I now try to make that an essential priority in my life. Stress can certainly be a culprit in how our bodies behave. I am challenged in the anxiety department, so I have to force myself to slow down and relax. Please evaluate your stress levels and put yourself as a priority. Give yourself permission to take care of yourself first. Only then can we effectively take care of others.

My challenge for you today is to consider pampering yourself a bit. Wherever you are, at least take slower breaths, book a manicure or a pedicure, take a long hot bath or schedule a massage or a facial. Whatever you can afford, please just put yourself first for a moment. It is the most selfless thing you can do. It makes you a much nicer person, and your family will love you for it.

MY CLOSET

Along with my love of makeup, I adore clothes. I have always dressed differently than most people I know. I have been accused of overdressing or trying to dress too wild, but I don't care. Shopping for the perfect outfit for the occasion has always been a passion of mine. The crazy thing is, although I am fully committed when I see myself in the mirror before an event, I sometimes cringe when I see photos of myself afterward and wish I had changed my clothing choice. I have always worn animal prints and bright colors.

A funny story, when Kennedy was in 2nd grade, I went to visit her at school for their Mother's Day program. I was appalled when her teacher told me that she couldn't wait to meet me because of what Kennedy had written about me. The kids were to write a paper on why they loved their moms, along with some drawings. The teacher then laminated them and made them into placemats for the luncheon. To my horror, Kennedy had put how much she loves when her mommy dresses up in her tight red dress and leopard shoes to go to work at night. Oh my gosh, kill me now! Obviously, she was referring to me dressing a bit more flashy for my concerts, but I can see how the teacher must have thought I might be a hooker. How embarrassing! Since then, I have tried to tone my look down a bit, to no avail.

I am now at the place in my life that what others think about my choices just doesn't bother me. I love unusual clothes. I love to stand out from the typical outfits you'd find off the racks. I have finally gotten to the point of being comfortable with being different. I was not born to fit in.

I am so proud that my passion for clothes must have passed down to my daughter Payton, who is now a well-known fashion stylist here in Nashville. The apple doesn't fall too far from the tree, I suppose.

My precious husband realized that a girl who loves

Kelly and her daughter Payton

fashion this much must need a noteworthy closet. He selflessly turned his office that he wasn't using into my glorious closet. I rarely let anyone in there as it is my private haven, but it's so pretty it seems such a shame not to share it with you. I put a beautiful chandelier above a well-organized island full of costume jewelry (another of my passions) and have sections of my favorite designers in certain areas. It is like my own personal store. I love Elizabeth Taylor, and I have a beautiful poster of her dressed as Cleopatra on my leopard print wall within.

When I was decorating this, I wanted to paint the back of the existing bookshelves a metallic gold to match the chandelier before any clothes were installed. I couldn't find a roll-on metallic, so spray paint it was. I tried a small part to see how it would look, and that encouraged me to complete the project. I waited till T.G. was out of town to really get busy spray painting the rest of the shelves.

Quickly realizing that I was breathing in too much gold paint, I tried to raise my windows, but they wouldn't budge. Halfway through finishing with the bookshelves, I ran out of spray paint and went to Lowes to buy more. The boy at the checkout asked if I was ok. I thought that was a weird question until I looked down at my golden feet. I went to the car and looked into the rearview mirror, and to my horror, I hadn't realized that the metallic paint had covered my entire face leaving me to look like an Academy Awards Oscar. Gold paint was completely covering my face, in my lashes, brows, and even up in my nose! I hurriedly came home and tried to wash it off, but it wouldn't budge. I did the best I could to remove it with baby oil.

Still needing to finish my paint job, I just kept going like an idiot. As I completed the last shelf, I began to get very dizzy and started to cough. I had trouble breathing. I embarrassingly took myself to the emergency room for inhalation problems. To this day, I think I have a residue of that paint still left in my throat. T.G. now calls me the woman with the golden voice. No regrets, though, as I have gorgeous, one-of-a-kind golden bookshelves for my shoe collection. One of T.G.'s favorite things about me is that it's never boring around our home. I am kind of like Lucille Ball, always getting into crazy things.

One bit of advice I can give about fashion is that you don't have to wear the most expensive or designer clothes to look put together. Although I love some designer things, my favorite is mixing and matching some less costly items with them. It gives you more of a unique look to not be so matchy-matchy from head to toe. I love a piece of statement jewelry, like a big ring or a tiny necklace. I am realizing lately that sometimes the smaller the piece, the bigger the impact.

People are always surprised to hear that I love shopping at consignment stores or even Goodwill for my eclectic finds. I have found some seriously high-end name brands by accident in those kinds of places. I don't like spending a lot of money on most of my clothes because I don't wear them more than a few times. When my pictures are taken in a certain outfit and put on social media, I most likely don't care to wear it again. I have been known to sell some clothes or donate them for charity and have also had requests to put some items into museums. I don't know if you are like me, but I get very attached to my clothes. They are like little friends to me. A certain outfit can bring back a memory for me from the event I wore it to. I sometimes mourn the loss of clothes if they get lost or torn. I know that sounds crazy, but hey, I still have my very first orange and white polka dot bikini from when I was one year old, along with my red chiffon dress (including my tiny white gloves) from my first beauty pageant at three!

About that pageant, the judge's final question to all of the contestants was, "What is your favorite food?" I froze and said, "Onions!" I have no earthly idea what made me say that as I seriously despise the taste of them. Needless to say, I didn't win the title of queen of the *Our Little Miss* pageant.

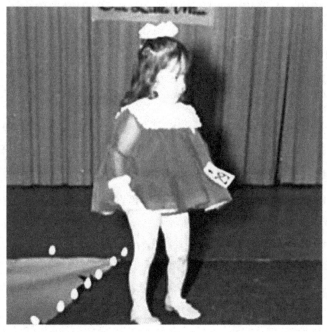

Kelly's first beauty pageant - three-years-old

I realize that this chapter might sound insensitive, and some might judge me for being materialistic or not appreciative of just having clothes on my back. I am aware of those not able to afford expensive clothes. I, too, have been there, so I think that's what makes me so grateful for them now. I feel so blessed when my friends look into my closet to *shop* for their special occasions.

If you find that you are not feeling like you are the best version of yourself, I encourage you to buy a new outfit or a pair of shoes. Try shopping at Goodwill. Try new styles. Expand your wardrobe, branch out, and try new makeup tips. If you just got an unexpected bonus, spoil yourself a little. Get that bag you have been dreaming of, within reason, of course. Make yourself a priority. I promise you will be glad you did.

I will say that I have learned that no matter how much you spend on makeup or a skincare serum, no matter what designer you may wear or how flashy your new purse is, inner beauty is the rarest and most precious jewel. I have seen some of the most outwardly beautiful people have such an ugly inside that it can change my perspective of their looks. Confidence is sexy. If you can just muster up enough spunk to enter the room with your head held high, no matter what you have on, people will find you super attractive.

Scan this code with your camera-equipped smartphone to view the bonus video. (Most IOS and Android devices can read QR codes by scanning with the built-in camera.) If you do not have a QR app on your phone visit your app store and search for QR code reader.

20

XOXO

I believe that laughter is the best medicine. Literally! After completing my treatments, I began to write with Lorrie Morgan and her keyboard player Mark. We met each week for almost a year to basically write Lorrie's life story to music. It was a wonderfully creative time for me and great to keep my mind occupied.

After one of our writing appointments, we were just hanging around the studio chatting. Lorrie mentioned that Fan Fair, or CMA Fest as it is now called, was coming up. This event is the largest gathering of country music fans, who come to Nashville for live music and sometimes meet their musical heroes. However, we both agreed that on occasion, a random fan would act as if they know more about an artist than they should, most of the time not having had all of their facts straight. For instance, someone may come up to Lorrie and call her by the wrong name or tell her they loved her song "I'm Looking for Something in Purple," when the actual title is "Something In Red." They will argue with you till you just give up. Every so often, these fans are also aspiring singers themselves.

I have no idea why I did what I did next, but I went home that night, gathered everything I have ever owned that might resemble a stage outfit, and planned to wear it to our next writing appointment and act out the role as a country music stalker. And so, right then and there, my alter ego, XOXO, was born. (Or as XOXO would say, *BORNED*).

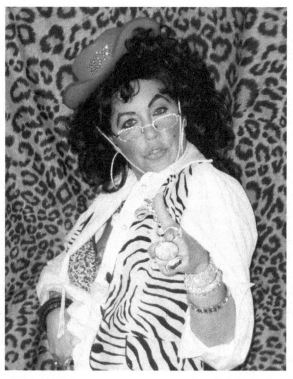

Kelly in charactor as XOXO

I spent hours giggling with T.G. and sometimes Lorrie just making up her crazy stupid back story. XOXO was borned Dewayna Sue in Bucksnort, Tennessee. She moved to Nashville and now lives in Jellybean Junction R.V. park, close to the Grand Ole Opry (just in case she needs to get there quickly should they call on her to perform). She has a daughter named Fallopia.

Dewayna Sue changed her name to XOXO as her stage name so people would never forget her. She drives a cooped-up pink Pacer and has been married seven times. Her choice of clothing is anything animal print (wearing all at the same time) and anything that sparkles WAY too much. Her hair is jet black, and she dons a tiny red cowboy hat with XOXO on the front in rhinestones, with a string underneath to hold her sagging chin in place. Her makeup, well, let's just say, it's a bit on the heavy side. You will always find her with a smudge of lipstick on her front teeth, eyebrows always too dark and uneven, and she has a beauty mark that seems to move every day. Some have accused her of it being a tick. She has way too much confidence on the verge of arrogance and has a bit of a naughty side. As you can tell, I had way too much time on my hands.

Each time I would put this outfit on, including her enormous belt buckle the size of a garbage can lid, something came over me. A funny side note is that the belt buckle was a gift given to my dad and passed down to me. If you look close enough, you can see LANG and tiny gold records with Conway Twitty's name engraved on it. When playing XO, I began to talk differently, walk differently, and I felt invincible. I would say things as this character that I would never be able to get by with as Kelly Lang. Those who know me very well know that I am actually more like XOXO in real life than the ladylike Kelly Lang the public gets to see most often. XOXO allows Kelly to

XOXO's extra large belt buckle

let her hair down and enjoy just being silly.

I would find myself lying in bed at night, thinking about her and giggling. I started to write music for her. Since she thought way too much of herself, these songs were so fun to create. For example, some of the titles are "Don't Hate Me 'Cause I'm Beautiful, I Was Borned This Way" Or the lyrics to her song "I'm Hot" goes like this:

I'm hot, hotter than a radiator in Dale Jr.'s car,
Yeh I'm hot, hotter than a tamale in Jose's bar.

Well, you get the drift. I recorded a series of songs horribly sung by this *Superstar*. I named the collection of her *Hits* and some fun stories in between, *Sex In The CD*. I later re-released a version with just the music as a project called *Sparkle And Twang*. I honestly just did this for fun. I dressed head to toe as her and struck a very cocky pose for the cover. It is wildly amusing to me that her music still sells very well from my website, www.kellylang.net, almost every week.

I began to thoroughly enjoy making little vignette

videos with my celebrity friends that you can now find on Youtube. XOXO has met Ricky Skaggs and his wife Sharon White in the grocery store, skated on the ice with Olympian Scott Hamilton, tried to climb William Lee Golden of the Oak Ridge Boys gates, and many more adventures. Everyone was a great sport, and I had a blast messing with people as this character. As the video views began to rise, I realized that something was catching on, whether I meant for it to or not. I even went through Caesars Palace in Las Vegas as XOXO, and called it *Caesars Salad*. People were excitedly stopping me for selfies. How crazy is that?

I began receiving fan mail from people all over telling me how much they enjoyed XOXO and how she made them laugh during their saddest of days. Most of them had already known my cancer story and that I had begun this character even though I had gone through a dark time myself. They would say that I was an inspiration or that it did their hearts good to belly laugh. Hmm, I didn't see any of that coming. One of the things I enjoyed doing the most as this character was sending birthday wishes or delivering someone a FaceTime message to lift their spirits.

One night, I played XOXO at *Ernest Tubb's Midnight Jamboree* and later turned myself back into Kelly Lang during the same show. I will admit, it's harder to do that than I thought. Taking off all of her garb proved to be quite a task, and then to look like a normal person afterward? *Wow!*

I likened XOXO to some of the characters that Cher would play on her TV show with Sonny Bono. I always loved the fact that she didn't take herself too seriously. I was also a big fan of Lucille Ball, Carol Burnett, and Gilda Radner. All of these women were fascinating and inspiring to me. I also thought it was cool that Vickie Lawrence was her own opening act as she played her *Mama's Family* character in her same show. Hats off to her, though. It's way more challenging than she makes it seem. Never in a million years did I ever think she would be anything more than something silly to play with; Boy, was I wrong.

To my surprise, Lorrie Morgan invited me to be her opening act at the Beau Rivage casino in Mississippi, and I was also an opening act at the Gold Strike Casino in Tunica, Mississippi, for T.G. The famous comedy club Zanies in Nashville invited me as an opening act for Killer Beaz, Reno Collier, and my favorite comedian, Leanne Morgan. Holy cow, had I opened a big ole can of worms!

A few years later, the Tennessean newspaper contacted me. I was flattered that they'd want to talk to me about my music career, but I was seriously shocked when they focused their story on XOXO. They wanted to highlight how her humor was healing for other breast cancer patients. The feature ran in an October issue highlighting breast cancer awareness month and was a huge story! I couldn't believe it.

I was then offered a mini-series on The Heartland Network, allowing me to film 13 five-minute episodes. This series included shows filmed with The Bellamy Brothers on a cruise ship, and with Larry Gatlin and John Rich in John's honky-tonk, Redneck Riviera. Broadway in Nashville was the perfect place for a broad like XOXO; both filled with glitz, glamor, and twang.

Shortly after, the Huckabee show invited me to make my national television debut. I was to storm the stage as an unwanted guest and sing my song "Sparkle and Twang." I made a point to call Governor Huckabee by the wrong name, *Hannity*. I then decided that my nickname for him would be Govy. I offered him some peanuts that I had kept in my cleavage as I needed them for my dropping blood sugar. As he was eating them, I told him that I had already sucked the chocolate off, and he spewed them out immediately. I put my sparkly boot up on his desk before a security man hauled me off stage.

Govy was such a great sport. He later told me that XOXO's appearance on his show was one of his highlights on air. As a matter of fact, I did make his highlight reel at the end of the season as they recapped the show. I was also later snuck into a box on his birthday episode and rolled out on the stage as a surprise gift for him. It was so much fun!

XOXO on the Huckabee Show

Although XOXO is on my website and is forever a part of my psyche, I don't play her as often as I should. I kid you not; every week or so, someone asks me about her. Eventually, when things slow down a bit in my music career, I may have time to bring her out of her dressing room more often.

My daughters threaten to bury me in her clothes when I die. I honestly think that'd be hilarious and would be flattered if they would. It's good to laugh and not take yourself too seriously. I sure don't.

Scan this code with your camera-equipped smartphone to view the bonus video. (Most IOS and Android devices can read QR codes by scanning with the built-in camera) If you do not have a QR app on your phone visit your app store and search for QR code reader.

21

ASCENSION

In January 2020, I was celebrating my 53rd birthday. I was thrilled that my friend and television personality Jim Norton and his partner Robert Walden had invited us to their beautiful estate in Jackson, Tennessee for a birthday dinner. He not only made an exquisite meal with a most unique dessert with dragonflies (he knows how much I love them), but he had invited a few of our mutual friends. I thought all of the guests had arrived, and then to my delight, I got a tap on the shoulder. I turned around to find that my precious friend Priscilla Presley had also come to surprise me! It was the week of Elvis's birthday, so for her to make the trek a few hours away from Memphis was quite an ordeal. Joining her was the CEO of Graceland, Jack Soden and his wife Leighanne, Pat Tigret, Dr. Jonathan and Nicholle Ellichman. and Dianne Norton. Funny thing, T.G. had been dear friends with the one and only Elvis. Who knew that all of these years later, Priscilla and I would become close. I had bright hopes for the year as we all did.

Kelly and Priscilla Presley

I had just received the news that Ascension Hospitals would be filming a commercial and using my song, "I'm Not Going Anywhere." On the way to my birthday dinner in Jackson, I was invited by Ascension associate Lauren Nelson to swing by the Ascension St. Thomas Midtown location to watch as they filmed the now infamous TV spot. There was a huge production crew shooting several scenes to connect within the commercial.

The magic of this ad was the fact that they used local Nashville doctors for the project. I was so happy to have their head of neurology within this commercial. He was so kind to visit outside in the hall with me about my song. When patients recognized their doctors in the images, it seemed to make an instant connection. One of the scenes was taken from a true story. It was about a homeless man who had always carried around a bible but could never read it due to his blindness. However, Ascension donated his first pair of glasses to him, enabling him to read his beloved bible. Watching the filming of this commercial all go down was like having an out-of-body experience; almost like seeing people playing myself in a movie role. All very surreal.

This all began a few months earlier when an email came from my music administrator, Blue Water Music Group. Ascension Hospitals wanted to know if I'd be interested in allowing them to use my song in their Nashville commercial. Oh, wow! I didn't see that coming. When something that special comes out of the clear blue, it is even more exciting!

After a few conversations with the folks at Ascension, we decided that it might be a good fit. We began negotiating and making plans to unite our publicity firms to coordinate the upcoming press to announce the new marketing campaign.

We signed the contract for my song to be used just in the Nashville region to test how it might resonate in *Music City*. How exciting it was to immediately get messages and texts from fellow music artists saying they happened to be in another room in their homes when the commercial would come on their screens. Several said they were stopped in their tracks and wanted to know who was singing that song.

An odd twist to this story: the song they chose for this commercial is the same song I had written 16 years before while watching my friend taking care of her sick husband and telling him, "Honey, I'm not going anywhere." These are also the same words of comfort that T.G. whispered in my ear when I needed to hear them the most. I honestly couldn't believe that they had chosen my song since their actual slogan is "Your Care Is Our Calling."

I asked my music administrator how Ascension could have known about my vintage song. She wasn't quite sure, but there had been whispers that they had heard me perform it in a Youtube video taken when I had sung it at the Bluebird Cafe in Nashville. Or perhaps it was from a video I made several years before as a promotional tool for my friend Nick Paranjape to encourage patients in the waiting room of Ascension hospitals. He wondered if I'd mind sharing my story. Of course, I was happy to do so. He and his small crew came out to our home in Hendersonville and set up their equipment. I was a tad bit nervous, as I hadn't shared my story intimately before and was worried about what they wanted to say to T.G. about this painful era. I was so grateful he was willing to share his experience from a loving partner's perspective. It is a priceless piece of my history now, but I didn't realize just how difficult it was on him. He said that most people don't realize that it's not just the patient that goes through cancer. The family suffers and worries right along with them. I felt bad that I honestly hadn't worried about how he might have dealt with my health crisis. He was always so upbeat and supportive. I never realized he had been hurt through the ordeal as well.

As Nick and his camera crew were leaving our home, he asked me if I could sing a verse of something uplifting that I had written to finish out the video piece. I thought for a minute and decided to pick up my white guitar out on our back patio and began to sing a bit of "I'm Not Going Anywhere."

I began to get several emails, texts and calls about this video from patients who had seen it while waiting for their doctor appointments. It was flattering for sure, but God had much bigger plans for this significant song.

I am not sure how it made it up to the top of Ascension's marketing team, Nick Ragone, EVP, Chief Marketing Officer, but I'm sure glad it did. Perhaps he saw them both.

I went into the studio with my dear friend Buddy Hyatt and laid down a new and better-produced piano version for them. It was just a very lush piano track with beautiful strings. They had been expecting to use the original version of this song that I had recorded many years before when I sang much higher, but I didn't want them to use that older version. We cut it down to a perfect 30-second and a 60-second spot. They were appreciative of how quickly I was able to turn in the edited and updated version.

On Jan 31, 2020, the beautiful and heartfelt commercial began to run. It was not only my mother's birthday but also Super Bowl Sunday! You would not believe how exciting it was to hear my song along with their gorgeous visuals every 15 minutes or so that night. My phone rang off the hook with people asking if it was me. I am amazed that anyone would recognize my voice at all! I was so excited when celebrity friends, whom I admired, would take the time to tell me how much they loved my song. Naomi Judd of the Judd's fame (whom I had worked with many years before as a child on the *Ralph Emery Morning Show*) reached out to tell me how proud she was of me. The incredible songwriter extraordinaire, Mac Davis, shared with me how good he thought the commercial was and how much he loved my writing. Other messages came from Richie

McDonald (Lonestar), Michelle Wright (Canadian Entertainer of the Year), and others. One of my favorites happened to be from Duane Allen from the Oak Ridge Boys. He called to say that this was a hit song equivalent to their monster song "Elvira." Now that's the ultimate compliment!

Kelly and Duane Allen of The Oak Ridge Boys

The marketing team at Ascension is brilliant. They placed their ad within the *Academy Awards* and the premiere of *Dancing With The Stars!* I was so proud! At the very end of the commercial, in tiny print it says, "written and sung by singer Kelly Lang, a former St. Thomas cancer patient." It's there, but the text is so little that I missed it the first few times that it came on.

Thanks to the phenomenon of modern technology, there is a cool tool on our iPhones called Shazam. If you've never heard of it, you are missing out! Have you ever been listening to a song, and you were scratching your head trying to figure out who on earth is singing it? Or what is the name of the song you're listening to? Well, ask Siri, "Who is singing this song?" and Siri will magically reply with both the artist and title - amazing! I had begun to be Shazamed so many times that I even made their charts! It's rather exhilarating to be Shazamed...more thrilling than being googled, that's for sure.

I was so very excited for the year 2020. All seemed hopeful to everyone. Of course, as we all know, that feeling of positive times ahead came to a screeching halt due to Covid-19.

The one thing I was so grateful for is that I could watch even more TV as we were stuck at home. Everyone watched more TV. I know this because every day, I would get several messages on Facebook, Instagram, Twitter, and my phone saying how many times they heard my commercial. Some said it was haunting them in their sleep. I loved it.

As the pandemic continued to prove to be even more serious than any of us had initially thought, the uplifting letters of support that people sent to me took on a more somber tone. I began to get messages from very despondent families saying they sang my song to their loved ones whom they had to leave in the hospitals due to Covid. Some played it on their phones for dear family and friends stuck in nursing homes to help comfort them. Unfortunately, I also heard from several that played it at their family's funerals.

Here is a small example of these precious messages that made their way to me:

"So Beautiful I just can't stop listening to these Anointing Words and Song. Thank You So much."
♥♥♥ - Jeanette W

"Such a sweet & poignant tribute song at a very appropriate time in our lives ......beautiful, heartfelt, & packed with so much love & understanding...being a nurse myself this song brought a tear to my eyes and I would like to take this opportunity to say "Thank You" to you Kelly for bringing it & Ascension Hospital to the forefront .... I have literally worn out my "Old Soul" CD and I am so looking forward to your Vol. 2 .... God Bless You Kelly Lang." - Peggy L

"This is the most beautiful song I have ever heard in my 71 years so, so beautiful and emotional it brings on tears every time I listen to it" ♥ - Donald W

Kelly, you do have a voice that is so soft and yet the words are so strong !! Such a Very Special Story that not only touched your heart as they spoke but to so many of us out here :) Thank you Kelly for being such an inspiration to all of us !!" - Marilyn M

"I'm fighting cancer right now and I know how you were feeling about not showing your weakness with your mate. It's hard to admit you need help. I know until I came to grips with it my wife struggled to get through to me that she was going to be here no matter

*how rough the road gets. Beautiful song Kelly It brings
me to tears but happy tears."* - Barry C

*"God is great. Thank you for this song as my mom went
through this also and we were all there for her. She
made it 25 years before we lost her so thankful."* - Jim F

*"WOOOOOOW! I cry so this story is really emotional.
When I listened to this song for the first time I cried.
Wonderful song no doubt."* - Elizabeth G

*"This is such a beautiful meaningful song. It reminds
us of the love of family and friends who have stood by
our sides through death, illness, and heartbreaks. But
to me, it also symbolizes the love Jesus Christ has for
us. He is with us no matter what we face in life. Your
beautiful voice delivers such a powerful message that
we all need right now."* - Tanya S

*"What a Blessing this song is. It brought tears to my
eyes and truly touched my soul. God Bless And Thank
You Kelly Lang for this song."*- Demmings V

*"Kelly, I heard your song 'I'm Not Going Anywhere
for the first time today. The lyrics, the tone,
the comfort, the inner peace, the inspiration,
everything about this song is just so calming and
healing that I think it is probably the best song
I've heard in a long time. Thank you, Kelly, for*

making us feel what God intends for mankind. Thank you, and, Thank you again." - Micah O

"I am currently going through Radiation and Chemotherapy for Colo-Rectal Cancer stage 3. Every day before my radiation starts, the radiologists, at my request, put "I'm not going anywhere" on the speakers for me to listen to. It is my motivation to get through this troubling time and to let my wife of 48 years know how strong our marriage and love for each other is. God Bless You for sharing this song with us....it means more than you will ever know." - Bob G

"Ms. Lang I would like to thank you for opening up and sharing your breast cancer journey. Your journey and your husband are really awesome! Thank you for releasing it. It has helped deal with my wife going to be with Jesus. I took care of her for about 9 months before she went to the hospital the last time.I never thought about leaving her! I wanted to do everything I could to make her life better, it just wasn't God's will. She was sick for over 2 years. I prayed for the Lord to take me instead of her. Now i understand why she went instead of me. Hearing your song has really brought peace to me. Again thank you for the music and your story. I pray this nasty disease doesn't return to you and that God would bless

you and T.G. in ways that you wouldn't expect."
- David O

As Covid continued to ravage our world, the nurses and doctors came to the forefront as our true heroes. I was so honored
that this song turned into an homage to them as well. It is such a
compliment to hear that it is compared to Debbie Boone's classic "You Light Up My Life," as it resonates with many different
situations. I just recently received a letter saying that someone
wanted to use this song at their wedding.

I was ultimately very moved that a few of the messages told
me that they began to find Christ after hearing the words to my
song, as He certainly isn't going anywhere.

Because of having so much extra time on my hands during
the pandemic, I began stretching my computer skills. I wanted
to put together a music video to depict the entire song instead
of just the 30 or 60-second commercial spot. I taught myself
how to make a video on iMovie. Although I could not make a
professional video due to Covid restrictions, I am super proud
of how it turned out. I am thrilled that it has played on so many
national TV interviews and gets tons of traction on my Youtube
page.

One day, out of the clear blue, I got a call from the Tennessee
Titans talent coordinator asking me if I'd be willing to sing the
National Anthem during October for Breast Cancer Awareness
Month. The Titans are sponsored by Ascension, and they felt
that this would be a good fit. Oh my gosh!!! How exciting/
terrifying! He asked me what size jersey I wore and what number
I wanted on it. I was quick to tell him that my favorite numbers

are 1111. So, that's what I got. 11 on the front and 11 on the back with LANG spread across my shoulders.

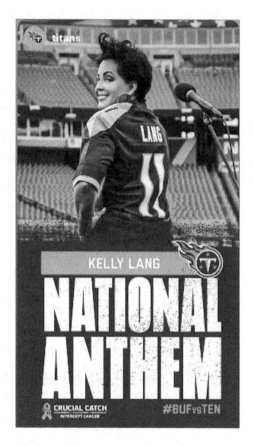

Due to Covid, the original game that I was to sing at had to be postponed for a few weeks until some players got better. If anyone has ever experienced the phenomenal opportunity of singing in a stadium, you will know that singing in a large bowl is very intimidating. It is challenging to be able to hear properly with the echo. I was secretly glad that they could pre-tape me singing without the audience in the stadium a day or so before the game so that I wouldn't be so scared. I was even more relieved that they decided to only play it at the stadium instead of airing it on national TV due to so many political stances surrounding the anthem. I am grateful for the link we were allowed to share on social media just to prove to myself that I actually did it. I think I went up a notch in the cool factor in my daughter Kennedy's eyes.

As the year progressed and the ravages of Covid-19 continued to prove more and more aggressive, the world seemed to feel even more defeated. When will this ever end?

Ascension realized that this commercial spot was a bit of a healing balm for the folks in the Nashville area, but they felt it could also be used as a source of comfort to the entire nation. They decided to make their newly modified commercial, only this time with masks, to all of their 22 markets which stretch across America, greatly expanding the awareness of my music to a larger audience. Here I was, not expecting this song to be heard at all, as it was created so many years before; now, I'm realizing an unexpected surge in my career. If I can be of encouragement to any other songwriter or anyone that creates something, please look at me as an example. God doesn't instill anything in us that we create in vain. Most of the things I have created in my life have sat on a shelf for many years. Then sometimes, 15 or more years later, they come to fruition. *DON'T GIVE UP!*

Another example of this very thing comes in the form of a children's lullaby project. When my oldest daughter Payton was only four years old, I wrote a series of nine songs for her. I called the collection of Christian/Country songs *Lullaby Country*. My talented, artist brother, Mike Lang illustrated the cover. I wrote it for her but soon realized that others began requesting them to give as baby gifts. This was so long ago when copies were made that they were in cassette form. Fast forward

15 years: an executive at Cracker Barrel got a hold of one of those cassettes and asked if I could make it into CD form because they wanted to sell them within their country stores! How exciting that was, yet it was short-lived. I honestly forgot all about the project for a very long time as I felt disappointed it didn't stay in the stores any longer.

With so much extra time on my hands, I took time to reflect on my life during the pandemic. I realized that if my song that I had created so many years before could make it into a national commercial, what other projects do I have sitting on the shelf that I could refresh for this new generation. Ah Ha! I re-released the *Lullaby Country* CD to a new digital format. It was so amazing that I had so many new opportunities that I had overlooked; I had to get quiet and still to hear God's prompting on what I could do. I just loved that so many women began to send me letters saying that they were excited to get this music for their babies or grandbabies because they had been sung to sleep by my music many years before. Always remember that nothing is created in vain.

Moving forward, since the Covid-19 restrictions have begun to lift, I am blessed to continue to perform all over the country in areas where the commercial airs. I am always so grateful when I begin to sing "I'm Not Going Anywhere," and the audience starts to sing the words back to me, some while tears stream down their faces.

I look very forward to a continued working relationship with the Ascension Hospital team in any capacity. Their Christ-centered hospitals are so compassionate, and I believe they are making such an extraordinary difference in how healthcare is done.

Scan this code with your camera-equipped smartphone to view the bonus video. (Most IOS and Android devices can read QR codes by scanning with the built-in camera) If you do not have a QR app on your phone visit your app store and search for QR code reader.

22

FROM T.G.'S PERSPECTIVE

I was in Memphis working in a medical company that my family and I owned when my phone rang. I knew that Kelly was going to be hearing from the doctor about her biopsy results. I had been on pins and needles, hopefully waiting for good news. However, I also had a sense of fear that was welling up inside of me that I might need to prepare for bad news as well. I said a silent prayer, "God, please let Kelly be ok."

I had this same sinking feeling of fear once before when my phone rang. It was the day that J.D. Sumner, Elvis Presley's bass singer, called. I knew something wasn't quite right as he had never called me before. He was calling to tell me that our friend Elvis had passed, but somehow I already knew. And I think I already had a fear that Kelly's call wasn't going to be a good one as well.

I answered the phone and heard Kelly's broken voice telling me, "T, I have cancer." I said, "Baby, I'm so sorry. I'm on my way home." The long drive gave me time to pray, cry and reflect on our relationship.

I had known Kelly since her teenage years, working with her professionally and knowing her father, whom I was in business with. I always thought the world of Velton and enjoyed our time together on the road with Conway. I've often wondered how he would feel about my having married his daughter. I would like to think that he would have approved. I frankly can not remember a time when Kelly wasn't in my life, almost like she's always been there. I thought back to the first time I became aware of her when I would sit in my kitchen drinking coffee as she performed on *The Ralph Emery Morning Show*. I loved her personality and talent and admired her passion for music. Down deep inside, I knew that she would somehow make a difference in the music industry.

I remember playing *Jamboree In The Hills* on my birthday on July 20, 1981, and seeing Kelly the day we both performed in front of 60,000 people. A picture was taken backstage of the two of us with her mom Nancy. That photo has since been made into a coffee mug and sits within our kitchen. To this day, when I am making coffee, I look into the cupboard and see the cup, and it brings me back to that special time. I look at it as a God wink letting me know that we were meant to be.

Another unusual thing that happened was when Kelly was the opening act for Mickey Gilley and me in Cookeville, Tennessee. Backstage that night, a photographer captured many pics of all who were gathered. Later, after Kelly and I had been married many years, she found all of those black and white photos from that evening. We couldn't believe that in one of the photos of us was both of our dads who have since passed. They were standing behind us as the picture was taken, almost as if they were watching over our union. That priceless picture is on our shelf within our music room today as a reminder that we were destined to be together.

T.G., Kelly and Mickey Gilley   *Cookville, TN concert poster*

Through the years, I have probably worked with hundreds of opening acts, but for some reason, every time Kelly was on the show, she stood out to me. She was unforgettable.

One of my favorite things about her is that you always know where you stand with Kelly. Her nickname is *Blunt Kelly*. I recall playing at Doc Severinsen's dinner club in Oklahoma City, Oklahoma. Kelly and her mom came to the show with their friend Louise. After the show, I invited them to visit with me on the bus. I asked if they'd like to hear my upcoming single, "War Is Hell On The Homefront." Her mom and Louise were very complimentary of the new music, but Kelly just sat quietly. I asked her if she liked it, and she told me that she wasn't a fan of story songs. I couldn't believe that this 15-year-old had such a strong opinion and wasn't afraid to share it. Her opinion has always meant the world to me, so her not liking my song was a bit hurtful. I tried to tell her that it would probably do very well for me on the charts, which it did, but she still holds strong to her opinion that it is not her favorite of mine. As much as I hated to hear that, I absolutely love her honesty and that she is not a *Yes* person.

A few years later, I was in the position to include Kelly as my guest on a show called *Fantasy*, an NBC production in L.A. hosted by Leslie Uggams and Peter Marshall. It showcased new talent that deserved a chance to be seen and heard on a national platform. I always believed in her talent and wanted her to have this opportunity. It was the first time we ever sang a duet. She did an incredible job, and I knew that she was destined for stardom. I was always happy to see her at musical events as she always had a smile on her face and lit up every room she would enter.

On my long drive home from Memphis, I asked myself this question. "What would my life be like without her?" I couldn't get home fast enough to hold her and tell her that everything would be alright. Kelly had always been the one to comfort me before when I was having a rough time. I was grateful to perhaps be a source of comfort for her now. She had a wonderful way of making me feel heard and important. When we first began dating, I remember telling her that I felt that the best part of my life was behind me. She just laughed and told me I was crazy. She made me believe that the biggest part was still in front of me. And once again, she was right. She challenged me to begin to live again, and for that, I'm so grateful. It was now my turn to give her that same gift in return. I had to show Kelly that the biggest part of her life was not behind her but in front of her. I am sure glad she listened.

Our relationship started off strictly as friends. For many years neither one of us looked at the other as a partner in life. After dating Kelly for some time, I realized that my happiest times were when I was in her presence. After a while, we became inseparable. Some would say we are connected at the hip, mostly because we have so much in common. We both have a love for God, travel, music, the same taste in homes, decor, and we both treasure our friends. I love that I can talk to her about anything. Since we are in the same business, I can share with her what I am experiencing on the road, and she completely understands because she entertains on those same stages. She is the perfect partner.

Memories of our relationship kept flooding back to me on that long drive back to Hendersonville. After arriving home, we began the dreaded journey through many tests, surgeries, chemo, and radiation. I stayed close by Kelly's side throughout each mountain we had to climb. I knew she needed me with her, but the truth is I love to be needed. I felt that it was my lot in life to take care of her. Some of my sweetest times were when she had treatments and stayed at her mom's

T.G., Kelly and Nancy Lang (Mom)
The Three Musketeers

home. I slept in the spare bedroom just to be near her as she recovered. I realized that the cancer made me feel closer to her during these dark days. She, her mom, and I became The Three Musketeers.

Although I knew that Kelly would lose her hair, I was still shocked to see the reality. To my surprise, she was just as beautiful with or without hair. It was my job to make sure she knew that truth. Her hair began to grow back in, and she wanted it to be as long as it was before. I, however, have grown to love the shorter, spikier look on her and encouraged her to keep it short. It fits her spunky personality even better than it ever did when it was long.

I truly love singing with Kelly and was very excited to record the album *Iconic Duets* with her. We learned a lot about each other during that time. I am more detail-oriented and have to read the lyrics line for line, but not Kelly. She just flies by the seat of her pants and seems to know the words to every song known to man. She drives me crazy, not seemingly prepared, but then she blows my mind with how effortless she ends up making everything work out for the best.

One of my favorite things about Kelly is, not only do I find her to be stunningly beautiful (it amazes me how much she looks like Elizabeth Taylor), but she is extremely funny. I laugh out loud every time I think of this next memory.

Kelly and I had been dating for a few months, and up until this night, she had only shown me the more serious, classy version of herself. After one of my shows at Bally's in Tunica, Mississippi, we decided to walk over to play a little blackjack. She had a beautiful white lace top on, and her long hair was pulled up into a braid. She was so feminine...but then, a gentleman at the end of the table asked, "Do you mind if I smoke?" Kelly didn't skip a beat. She replied instantly, "Why no, do you mind if I fart?" *YOU'VE GOT TO BE KIDDING ME!* I asked, "Did she just say what I think she said?" The blackjack dealer just giggled and said, "Yep, that's what she said!" I knew right then how much fun she was going to be. I can honestly say that life with her is never, ever boring. People ask me how I feel about her crazy character XOXO. They can't imagine that I would like my beautiful wife dressing up to be so awful looking, but the truth is I thoroughly love that she doesn't take herself too seriously. We laugh about something almost every day.

Kelly has been through a lot of pain in her life. I feel that it is my job to make sure the rest of her life is pain-free and filled with as much happiness as possible. Although I have had many wonderful titles bestowed upon me, my most cherished ones are being a husband to Kelly and a father to our children.

I have always believed in God, but since being with Kelly, I have become much more spiritual and love having a personal relationship with Him. One of my favorite things to do with Kelly is to pray daily for our friends and thank Him for so many wonderful blessings in our lives. I always ask Him to validate Kelly and her career. She is so deserving. I am beyond proud of her accomplishments. Kelly is one of the most talented people I've ever known, so kind, and has a heart of gold. I am honored to be her husband. I see how her life has turned around and how many people her life affects like she has mine. My prayer is this book will positively help someone as much as she has helped me. I love just living in her radiant presence.

I am amazed that I have learned so many lessons from her, being that she is so much younger than me. Kelly has taught me to stop and smell the roses, not to take life too seriously, and to appreciate every detail of my day. We are not promised tomorrow, so enjoy it now, and with whomever you adore today.

A note to all men reading this book: I want to encourage you to cherish your spouses in good times and bad. In hindsight, what some would consider being the hardest days of our lives (and they were hard) were actually some of the sweetest memories. The bad times helped us grow closer as partners. It was like glue for us. It is sometimes a difficult choice to stay and support our women, and, believe me; I am aware that some men simply don't stick around. But, let me assure you that there will be blessings that will flow abundantly over your relationship if you do.

I also realized a big lesson that when your partner has cancer, you also experience the effects of the disease, but in a different way. Although it isn't the same pain as the patient, I guarantee that I was in a lot of emotional pain just watching her suffer. I so appreciate all the friends and family that reached out to support us at that time as a couple.

I have no idea what God has in store for us, but I'm excited to see what He has planned for our future. At the time of my writing this chapter, Kel and I have been together for almost

21 years. I am proud of that. I love being her partner, and I look forward to many more years with her to come.

Kelly and T.G. - Happily Ever After

Scan this code with your camera-equipped smartphone to view the bonus video. (Most IOS and Android devices can read QR codes by scanning with the built-in camera) If you do not have a QR app on your phone visit your app store and search for QR code reader.

23

MY BABIES

Writing about my daughters is like describing two parts of myself that just happen to live outside of my body. They are very, very different, but strangely, exactly like me at various times in my life. If I were to get a big pair of scissors and cut myself in two, you could see me in each of them. Don't tell them!! They would deny that at all costs!

My oldest daughter Payton just turned 30 while I was completing this book. I can't believe I have a child that age! Oh, how much wiser and braver she is than I ever was. My heart burst with pride as I see her raise money for charities that are close to her heart. She loves her friends fiercely, she donates her time to take foster girls shopping for new clothes to help them with their confidence, and she is devoted to helping others see their best potential with her significant work as a well-known clothing stylist.

Anything I am not sure of, I just call her, and she has already done the research and gives me well-educated advice. So strange to learn so much from your child. She lives in Nashville, is married to Tobin Dale, and is the mother of my two grand puppies, Bo and Arrow.

My youngest daughter Kennedy (26) just got married to Zack Jones and is the mother of my 3rd grand puppy Chipper. They Live in Hendersonville and plan on starting up a Bed and Breakfast. She is super athletic and was a star soccer player, even getting a scholarship to play in college. I love how much she loves children, and I see her having a few of her own. She threatens to have them call me *Glam-Mother*. Oh well, I guess there are worse names.

Kennedy is very intuitive and feels for people around her. I love how she also picks up the tabs of elderly people she may see in a restaurant. She is a great friend that gives very blunt advice (I guess she may get that from me, but hey, you always know where you stand with us).

Kelly and her girls (L) Payton (R) Kennedy

I am equally proud of them and am thrilled to be their mother. They are both wildly independent young women, just as I'd hoped they'd be.

At the beginning of the book, I mentioned the fact that my oncologist advised that I might want to write my girls a letter in case I didn't make it through cancer. In hindsight, I'm glad I didn't take her advice. I wanted to think more positively, and I feel that this book of hope and accomplishment is what I'd like to leave to them as my legacy. My wish is that one day they can look back on my life and, within the pages of this book, know more about me than before and know how much their mamma loves them.

Payton, Kelly and Kennedy

Scan this code with your camera-equipped smartphone to view the bonus video. (Most IOS and Android devices can read QR codes by scanning with the built-in camera) If you do not have a QR app on your phone visit your app store and search for QR code reader.

HOPE IS ON THE HORIZON

24

As of the printing of this book, I am very grateful to be almost 17 wonderful years out from that dreaded date of my diagnosis. I've learned many valuable lessons along the way.

I am happy to say that both of my amazing daughters are now married and doing great in their lives. My beautiful mom is 83-years-old and healthy. T.G. and I have been together for 21 years. That's like 1,000 years in the music business!

Kelly's Family

I feel like I have come light years from being that insecure little girl at the beginning of my story until now. I sincerely love where I am in life. I know most people wish they could go back to a certain age when they were younger, but not me. I may have made other choices than I did at the time, but then again, I wouldn't be where I am today if even one life decision was different. I have no regrets. I love this age in my life (54) because I now can look back over things in my journey that didn't work out the way I planned and see why. I clearly can see that God had a different and much better path than I had thought for myself.

Watch "Kickin' It With Kelly" on YouTube

It is amazing to now have the perspective to look back and see how the web was woven into a beautiful masterpiece that I could not have spun myself. Because of that wisdom, I can relax more into my life and feel much more secure than I did when I was younger. I am still working on my confidence as a woman. Some people may think that I have it all together; I assure you I do not. Nobody does! That's the thing...as soon as I realized that no one ever really has it all together, I was able to feel comfortable with the idea that I wasn't supposed to be perfect. I was so hard on myself before, and still am, according to friends; but I am learning to be ok with not always being ok.

There are a few tips I've learned along the journey that help me keep my otherwise very crazy life more calm and normal. Incorporating them into the way I think has helped me not take myself too seriously, not be so insecure, and how to see things more clearly. Here they are:

Tip 1. Be Mindful Of How You Speak

Speak kindly over others and yourself. Speak with integrity. Say only what you mean. Avoid gossip about others. Use the power of your words to spread kindness, truth, and love. Try not to cuss or say ugly words to people. Especially, don't talk bad about yourself. Learn to quieten that small voice that is always trying to tear you down.

Tip 2. Don't Take Anything Personally

Nothing others do is because of you. What others say and do is a projection of their own reality, their own dream. When you are immune to the opinions and actions of others, you won't be the victim of needless suffering. If someone says you are ugly, that is just their opinion. It's not the truth. The same thing when someone tells you that you are beautiful; it is also not the truth. It is just their opinion. I have learned to live more neutral in the fact that I don't let other people's opinions affect me anymore. By using this tool, I don't take any compliments or cut downs personally. When someone tells me that I am talented, it is just the same as if they said, "You have green eyes." I didn't do anything to get the talent, so how can I take that to heart? I just say thank you. It's not that I don't appreciate a kind word, it's just that I don't trust the sincerity.

When I see haters on social media, this tip has taught me not to take that to heart either. I just wouldn't want to be them. People that write mean things in their basement behind the screen are usually very unhappy themselves.

Tip 3. Don't Assume Anything

With just this one mindset, you can completely transform your life. Think of it like this. Don't assume the worst if someone didn't call you back when you think they should have. They may have gotten sidetracked with a family member, or their phone may have died. It's more than likely nothing like you have made up in your head when someone doesn't text you back. They may be in the middle of something and haven't seen the message yet. Be calm and know that what you're assuming probably isn't true. Time will tell.

Tip 4. Always Try To Do Your Best

Your best will change from moment to moment; Some days, you will feel better than you do other days, so your best may look different from day to day. If you know you've done your very best, you can lay your head on your pillow better at night. By simply doing your best, you will avoid self-judgment, self-abuse, and regret.

Tip 5. Listen To Your Inner Voice

I've learned to really listen to that small inner voice (I think it is the Holy Spirit) that guides me, so I don't make quite as many or as big of mistakes as I did when I was younger. It can protect you from getting into dangerous situations. For instance, if you feel uneasy about getting into an elevator with a stranger, just take another one. You don't need to apologize for taking the next ride.

About that inner voice: A few times in my life, I have experienced something very cool I want to share with you. I was concerned about sharing this because I didn't want to sound weird, but it has transformed my life. I hope this info will help you too.

When my mom was 72 and had been a widow for almost 13 years, she finally told me she was lonely. She wanted me to help find her a companion. *OH GREAT!* Mom, you've narrowed down your playing field a bit! She wanted me to put her on a dating website. I was worried, but I reluctantly helped her. After a few days, I got very nervous. My family would be so mad if they knew that I had fixed her up with strangers. I told her that we needed to get her off of that site and that if God wanted her to have a companion, He would send her one.

A few days later, I was at my daughter Kennedy's soccer game. I sat on the visitor's side so I wouldn't have to deal with my ex and his family, but I still wanted to support her. At the end of the game, something weird happened to me. I looked up, and walking towards me was a man that looked identical to my father, maybe how he would have looked if he were a few years older. The thing that I recall being so weird, though, was that the closer he came to me, the entire stadium began to blur, and he became more in focus. All of the faces were a complete blur but his. I am not one to just walk up to a complete stranger, so the fact that I did was an out-of-body experience in itself. I felt almost pushed off of the bleacher seat to go and speak to him. I

asked him his name, and he told me it was Paul Jackson. Hmm...
I didn't know what else to say except, "Wow, you look just like
my dad, who passed away years ago, and that's a compliment!"

A few days later, I got an email from him. His granddaughter
played on Kennedy's soccer team, and her dad told Paul who I
was and who I am married to. Paul decided to Google me and
found my website. He said it was great to meet me and that he
was sorry that he hadn't recognized me. He mentioned that
he loved both mine and T.G.'s music and to please say hi if we
saw him again. He also included his picture within the email.

I immediately sent this to my mom. You know what she
said? "Oh Kelly, I've already *winked* at him on Seniors.com!"
Of all of the places for Paul to have been from, he only lived
about 30 minutes from my mom. We set them up the next day
for lunch at the Cracker Barrel, and they've been together for
over 11 years now.

T.G., Kelly, Nancy Lang and Paul Jackson

I don't tell you this story to brag about my ability to be
a great matchmaker. I do want to emphasize that in my life,

whenever I look back, I can pinpoint the exact time that God wants me to meet someone who will be important in my journey. Everyone and everything goes blurry, and the one I am to focus on becomes crystal clear. Literally!

I would like to share a story with you about another memorable time that this has happened and (I want it on record that I have TOTAL permission from the person it is about). I was in the Nashville Palace watching a musical show. It was a benefit for someone I didn't know at the time. I only went to support my friend Scott Sexton who was putting on the event and the sponsor for the evening was Gus Arrendale from Springer Mountain Farms Chicken.

Scott Sexton is not only my dear friend but has turned into my full-time Public Relations Manager. Any time anyone is in need, Scott is always the very first in line to help. What a kind, honest and loving heart he has. T.G. and I are honored that Scott has chosen us to host his annual benefit Country For A Cause.

T.G., Gus Arrendale, Scott Sexton and Kelly

Gus is very generous to back so many events and projects in the music business. I am so grateful and honored to not only have his support in my career, but more importantly to have him as a precious friend. Springer Mountain Farms Chicken is the best chicken on earth. If you haven't tried it, I recommend you run, don't walk to your nearest grocery and buy some. You'll thank me later.

As the evening ended, I was just standing around, not really paying attention to too much going on. I saw T.G. visiting with Gus, and since I had already said my hello's and goodbye's, I was standing off to myself, ready to leave. Lo and behold, that blurry thing began to happen. The entire room went fuzzy except for one young lady about 20 feet away. She was crystal clear. I thought, "Oh no, here we go again!"

The message I was being nudged to share with her felt so strange. I heard God tell me to go and encourage her. I had no idea why. I reluctantly walked over to her and told her about my breast cancer journey and that whatever she was going through, she would be fine. I don't recall the exact words. I didn't even know that she was the one they had the benefit for that evening, but God knew. I honestly never thought I'd ever see her again. I didn't even ask her name.

This person later reached out over social media telling me her name was Kim Fannin, and how much my encouragement meant to her. She had been having a very blue time in her life as she too had been battling breast cancer. Kim shared with me that my words lifted her spirit. I was glad I was able to brighten her day but didn't think much more of that. About a year later she confided in me that her life situation seemed so very dark that she had seriously planned on taking her life the very next day, and if I hadn't intervened the night before, she wouldn't be here now. *WOW!* I realized then and there how important every word we speak or action we take not only affects us but can be life, or in this instance, death-altering. I am so very grateful God was able to use me for good that evening.

Kim Fannin is one of the most generous people I've ever met and my life has been blessed beyond measure by knowing her. She challenges me to be a much better version of myself. We have since become extremely close friends and enjoy lifting one another up each day. What a lovely friend she is to help celebrate my wins and she is always there to help comfort me during my losses.

She and I now share family members being that we have dogs that are sisters, Piper and Coco. I am so grateful that I heeded God's nudge, or I would have missed out on not only her friendship but the pack of women friends that she has shared with me, who I never even knew I needed.

Kim Fannin and Kelly   *Coco and Piper*

Something I realized along the way is, when your world gets super blurry, that's when God clears your vision for what He really wants you to focus on. These are only a couple of examples. Things like this happen to me all of the time. Not because I am special, but because I am keenly aware of how to hear Him. We all have this ability. The more in tune you are with hearing Him, the easier it is to recognize. When you feel the urge to lift up someone, please do it. It just takes a second for you to compliment someone, but that kind word will last a lifetime for the person you spoke with.

Speaking of blurry, I want to talk about something that I went through as a child, which still affects me to this day. I was born legally blind. My vision was 20/200 in one eye and 20/400 in the other. Until I showed signs at school of poor vision in the 3rd grade, I never saw separate blades of grass or leaves on trees, rather less a bird in the sky. I began wearing glasses at that time but then progressed into contacts as I began to perform. The only problem with contacts is they never fit correctly due to a severe astigmatism I had.

I was so happy to be a candidate for the new radial keratotomy eye surgery that I signed up for at 18. Funny story, after surgery, I was told to take my bandages off after 3 hours of sleep. I was too scared. Mom called the doctor to have him coax me to remove the bandages off of my eye. I reluctantly peeled it off and was horrified that I was blind, as I couldn't see a thing, and my eye was still numb. He laughed and said, "Now, Kelly, take the tape off of your eyelid." How embarrassing! I didn't even realize my lid was taped down. I cried tears of joy as I was only then able to see the sweet details of my mother's beautiful face. I was able to see 20/20 for the first time. What a miracle!

Isn't that kind of like life? Sometimes we need someone else to help us see better, and sometimes we just need to take the stupid tape off of our own eyes to see things more clearly. As I matured, after 25 years, as we all do, I needed reading glasses. I hated to have to go back into contacts again, but I am so very thankful for the years I spent enjoying perfect vision. Some people are surprised to hear that I deal with glaucoma, requiring drops each day. I am just so thankful for the opportunity to see life more clearly.

Kelly and Elizabeth O'Connell

I've really learned to cherish my friends. I have friends from all walks of life, and they are equally important to me. I still have some of my most cherished friends from childhood, where I grew up in the most amazing neighborhood called Bluegrass Estates. My sweet girlfriend Elizabeth O'Connell, whom I've known from that neighborhood since 3rd grade, always has my back, and I have hers. I take great pride in how long we've stayed close all of these years later. She is like a touchstone to me of where I came from; she's always there to support any of my crazy hair-brained ideas. Although I remain friends with most of the neighborhood kids, life happens, and unfortunately, we don't get to see each other as much as I'd like. Thank goodness for Facebook! As my career has evolved, I have met new friends along the way, and I always enjoy meeting more. You can't have enough as far as I'm concerned. A good friend is invaluable. If you struggle meeting new people, just open your heart for that to come your way. Be brave and strike up a conversation with a complete stranger; you never know, you may meet your new best friend today. That's how I look at people now.

Who knows where God will direct my path in the future, but I know I now can get through anything. When I am asked what my 5-year goals are, I can excitedly say that I hope to continue on the exact path I am on today. I plan to reach more people with my story of hope, and I plan to use my platform to help make a difference. I am doing more speaking engagements to connect with people's hearts.

I hope to remain healthy and strong. I am working on learning to cook, eating better, and working out a little more. I don't enjoy exercising, but I do love pilates. I have a long way to go and hope that I have the time it takes to be more comfortable in those areas.

These days, I spend as much time as I can in my swimming pool. Everyone teases me about my obsession with the weather forecast. If it is warm outside, I will forgo any plans I have to bask in the sun.

When I'm not in the pool, I love to spend as much time as I can in the studio making music. I am happiest when surrounded by incredible musical geniuses. I liken the musicians we work with as skilled surgeons, the very best Nashville has to offer. One of the things I enjoy the most is producing my own albums as well as other artists. It is like painting a beautiful scene on a blank canvas to hear the songs come alive.

At the time I am writing this book, I am currently recording a new album of vintage rock songs called Old Soul II. I am also excited to be writing new material for an upcoming original album. It is exhilarating to be able to record my words and melodies with an open heart, not knowing where they will end up one day. I don't write with an agenda. I listen to what God sends my way and try to be obedient to His direction for the individual song. I feel my best songs come when there is not a lot of pressure riding on a deadline. I've recently enjoyed going back through some of my older catalogs and re-recording some songs with more current sounds, and finding them to be a good fit for television projects. Who knows, I may even continue to write some crazy new tunes for my old girl XOXO and bring her out into the daylight a little more often.

I have been fortunate to travel professionally and for fun, and I still look forward to seeing all of the places I have hanging on my wish board. I sure hope this world opens up for future travel abroad. My hope is that I'd love to bring T.G. back to visit Switzerland with me to see the majesty of the Alps. We had a trip planned before the pandemic to go there, but that dream was obviously halted. I also began to realize during lock down, that there are so many gorgeous places right here in the United States that I've yet to visit. I am determined to see the Redwood Forest and explore the beauty of the east coast as well.

Eventually, I'd love to live on the beach. I wrote a song called "Down In Destin." about how much I love Destin, Florida. I see myself retired there relaxing, overlooking the gulf with a cup of coffee and painting, with a white terry cloth robe and a towel on my head. Don't ask me why; it just seems super glamorous.

I will say that as a summary of what I've been through with having had cancer, my life since that experience has been nothing but miraculous. However, trust me, I am sensitive to the fact that not everyone's journey is the same as mine. I know that the trials are much harder for many, and for some, they sadly end too soon. Sometimes I felt guilty for being alive, and I actually dealt with survivor's remorse. After a while, I realized that in doing so, it was not serving God's purpose for my life in the way it should be. As time passed, I remembered reading about how the Japanese put broken pottery pieces back together with gold. Very much like our Heavenly Father shows us that by embracing our flaws and imperfections, we can create an even stronger and more beautiful piece of art, called our lives. I built upon that principle and took the scars that cancer had brought into my life, humbly accepting God's healing and mercy as He filled in my broken pieces. That moment is when I decided God has a plan for each one of us and that I needed to get out of my own way and let Him do His work through me. I do not write this book or share the stories of my healing to be boastful in any way. Quite the contrary, I feel extremely blessed to have married the man of my dreams and to have seen my children grow. I am so thankful to have sung on the greatest stages with some of the biggest international stars and to have traveled the world. Of all of these wonderful experiences, the thing that fulfills me most is being able to use my story to help others. Through my words within this book, I hope that maybe a song I have written or performed has brought someone a blessing. Who knows, I hope I live long enough to write another book filled with even more life experiences to share.

Till then, "I'm not going anywhere."

God bless you all,

Scan this code with your camera-equipped smartphone to view the bonus video. (Most IOS and Android devices can read QR codes by scanning with the built-in camera.) If you do not have a QR app on your phone visit your app store and search for QR code reader.

A BIG THANK YOU TO:

Gus Arrendale of Springer Mountain Farms Chicken
for sponsoring my story and other endeavors in my
career. Your kind support allows me to dream bigger
and gives me the opportunity to have my music more
broadly known. Above all, I am forever grateful for your
friendship.

Kim Fannin, thank you for encouraging me to write
my story, and believing that it might help others. I
appreciate your input and love and I am so grateful for
your friendship. Just knowing you has made my world a
brighter place and I love you.

Jacy Dawn Valeras for believing in and encouraging me
to be the best version of myself. Thank you for working
so hard with me to help me reach my goals. You're such
a wonderful friend and I am blessed to have you in my
life. You are loved.

Scott Sexton, my publicist, but more than anything, my personal cheerleader. Thank you for always keeping my eye on the prize.

Buddy Hyatt for speaking positivity into my heart about my talent. You have been very influential in my sound, and have given me more confidence to be myself behind a microphone.

Nick Ragone from Ascension Hospitals for choosing my song "I'm Not Going Anywhere" in your campaign. Your heart of compassion towards the patients and in honoring your doctors and nurses is unsurpassed.

Missy Querry for your tireless dedication to this project and hard work to get my story edited properly for others to see. Your belief in me is unlike anything I've ever known, and I will never be able to repay you.

For More Information
visit
KELLYLANG.NET

Connect With Kelly

facebook.com/kellylangmusic
twitter.com/kellylangmusic
instagram.com/kellylangmusic

Listen and Watch

ABOUT THE AUTHOR

There are many sides to Kelly Lang: a singer/songwriter, oil painter/artist, record producer, comedian, speaker/ spokesperson, author, wife, singing partner of country music legend T.G. Sheppard, and most importantly, a breast cancer SURVIVOR.

Growing up in country music, her father, Velton Lang, was the long-time road manager for Conway Twitty. Being around great legends in the music business gave Kelly the desire to pursue a career in music.

Her love and passion for music is the thread that continues throughout her career. As an artist, Lang has released several albums, including *11:11, Shades of K, Throwback, Obsession, Iconic Duets* with husband, TG Sheppard, a classic children's album *Lullaby Country,* and *Old Soul.*

As a songwriter, she continues a stellar career having songs recorded by artists such as Ricky Skaggs, Lorrie Morgan, The Oak Ridge Boys, Crystal Gayle, George Jones, B.J. Thomas, Jimmy Fortune, Jerry Lee Lewis, TG Sheppard, and Johnny Lee to name a few. Lang has also performed/recorded duets with Sir Barry Gibb, Dame Olivia Newton-John, Paul Shaffer, and Lee Greenwood.

As part of a national campaign, Kelly's voice and writing skills shine in her song "I'm Not Going Anywhere" throughout the United States as the official anthem for Ascension Hospital's television commercial.

Originally from Oklahoma City, Oklahoma, she calls Hendersonville, Tennessee, home since moving there as a child.

VISIT
KELLYLANG.NET/MUSIC
TO EXPLORE THE
MUSIC COLLECTION
OF AWARD-WINNING
SINGER SONGWRITER
KELLY LANG

KELLY LANG